INVESTING IN THE 70'S

INVESTING

IN THE 70'S

Profitable Approaches for
Middle-Income Investors

DAVID L. MARKSTEIN

Thomas Y. Crowell Company   New York   Established 1834

Designed by Virginia Smith

Manufactured in the United States of America

L.C. Card 72–78269
ISBN 0–690–45001–X

1 2 3 4 5 6 7 8 9 10

CONTENTS

INTRODUCTION

In the 1950's and until fairly late in the 1960's, it was easy to make money as an investor. It was plausible for the author of one financial book to write that people should buy stocks to go up because they had always gone up. And, for a time, they did, enforcing the belief of many investment advisers that any day was a good day to buy stocks, that growth stocks would keep on growing forever, and that the investor who bought a future IBM (everything new was touted as a future IBM) would fare as well as the lucky ones who bought the real IBM long ago and watched their stakes steadily rise. But even IBM, sound as it was, ceased rising when the bubble began to break and harder market times came around.

Those simple, happy days when everyone could make money buying stocks ended with the 1960's.

There will be opportunities again—there are opportunities now. These may not glitter as did the scientific stocks in 1965, the hamburger stocks in 1968, or the housing stocks in 1969, but they exist. The purpose of this book is to help you find them in a new decade when investing will be harder but still profitable.

Chapter 1 tells how the balloon burst—how the frenzy for "growth" investments puffed itself up until it went bang! And there were the growth stocks, littering the exchange floors and costing innocent investors who had come to believe in growth forever part—sometimes all—of the money with which they started.

Chapter 2 postulates a business background which is not cheery. There will be harder times than most people knew during the sixties and fifties. Inflation, sometimes contained and sometimes flaring out, will be a continuing fact of life. The dollar is likely to stay in trouble; there will be new crises and problems which cannot be cured by Washington jawboning or talked away by blaming other nations. Even against this bleak background, it is possible to achieve investing success.

Chapter 3 examines new approaches to stock valuation. It looks at the entries on the balance sheet and the quick-assets yardstick which indicates true undervaluation. It explores a technique—little known but available to all—for finding out what knowledgeable corporate insiders are doing so that you can invest with them, selling when they see sufficient trouble to unload their holdings, buying when they are optimistic enough to add to their stock positions. It shows what is important and what is superficial in the insider buying data. A meaningful approach neglected during the frenzy for growth is the measurement of assets in the ground; this is discussed in Chapter 3, along with a technique for finding fast movers that shoot up quickly (and often decline as quickly).

Blue chips in place of blue sky is also discussed in Chapter 3. While the growth madness lasted, investors avoided blue-chip stocks representing the biggest situations in basic industry. They looked for small companies to which a successful new product might mean a doubling of earnings. They learned that the mistake which a big company can shrug off wrecks the little-growth outfit. This section on blue-chip investing examines past market phases of blue-chip favor (usually when the hangover from a growth binge makes stock buyers cautious) and explains the important principle of interest rotation—the technique which puts you in a blue-chip stock only during its time of high favor, moving along to fresh interest areas as these revolve into high regard.

Some mutual funds made a mess of things during the growth frenzy. Too many—but not all of them—manipulated asset values with questionable letter stocks or bought performance issues which performed only downward. Nevertheless, mutuals continue to have a place in intelligent investors' plans. Chapter 4 shows the variety available. It indicates relative advantages and drawbacks of open-end and closed-end funds and suggests ways to judge a fund for ability to produce high income, build capital gains, or hold invested capital safe.

Bonds were the Orphant Annies of the fifties and sixties, but they can be stellar performers in the new investing atmosphere of the seventies. The income approach can produce capital gains as well as high immediate living if a plowback technique—explained in Chapter 5—is followed. This chapter examines convertibles, shows when bonds are best purchased "flat" or at a discount. Bond ratings are explained with applicability to both straight and convertible issues. At times, if an investor judges wisely, he can achieve capital gains in bonds greater than are possible in common stocks.

An investor needs sources of information and advice. From a broker? A professional adviser? The statistical services which specialize in gathering facts without expressing opinions on the meanings and probable significance of the facts and figures? Chapter 6 examines information and advice sources, shows possible bias and degree of objectivity of each, and counsels ways to rate them. It gives tips on keeping commissions low, an important consideration in a day when thirty to forty in-out transactions can eat up all of an investor's starting capital in commission charges.

Not everyone has sizable sums to invest, and the background of potential recession—even depression—does not make it any easier for most investors to accumulate capital. The answer lies in leverage. Chapter 7 explains this and examines ways to make one dollar do the work of two, and even of four and five dollars, in intelligent speculation. It goes into simple margin, options such as warrants, puts and calls, points out how to add extra leverage to the already large leverage of warrants, shows the borrowability of convertible bonds or preferreds which can be traded as common stock with less money (producing greater income in many cases). Leverage is built into certain corporations' capital structures; you're shown how to seek and use these to best advantage.

Chapter 8 goes into opportunities not found in the United States and points out how to judge the merits of foreign securities on which less information is normally available than can be had on domestic stocks and bonds. Included are: The offshore mutual fund; American Depositary Receipts as a way of owning foreign stocks without becoming entangled in foreign treasury and other legal regulations; the multinational corporation; and bank deposits in Switzerland and other nations.

Chapter 9 tells you how to employ money profitably for short terms when the outlook is sufficiently clouded and sound judgment says to sit on the sidelines and wait. It goes into ways to buy a bank Certificate of Deposit on most favorable terms; Treasury Bills; tax-exempt short-term paper and how its place depends upon your tax bracket; bonds with close-in maturities and high yields; and how to use commercial paper even if an investor cannot invest hundreds of thousands of dollars at a clip.

Plans for affluent retirement are discussed in Chapter 10. It suggests ways to avoid the plight of the retiree who envisioned luxury in a $100-a-month seaside cottage, with a nickel newspaper and groceries at 1962 prices. It explains the dollar-averaging plan which brokers have taught many investors to regard as a statistical path to assured success. (It isn't.) It also goes into other investment formulas which look good on paper or when charted backwards into the known past, but which work less well when applied to an unforeseeable future. You will read about a Keogh plan for the self-employed and the advantages and drawbacks of a professional corporation or a living trust.

Will the present rules apply tomorrow? Chapter 11 tells how Wall Street has changed *and how you can benefit*. It discusses the passing of brokers' emphasis on serving an average investor and their growing bows to institutions. These accounted for 20 percent of the trading activity five years ago and now bring about 70 percent of an average day's trading on the New York Stock Exchange.

Whether dominated by institutions or millions of little investors, the market is subject to slips, stumbles, and falls. Chapter 12 tells how to avoid Papa Bear markets. It spells out a number of plans proposed by experts for spotting market turns.

Real Estate has been the traditional producer of great fortunes. Like the stock market, real estate will work under new rules. Chapter 13 discusses the changed conditions for investing in land, bricks, and mortar.

"Tax shelters" take the form of buying limited partnerships in petroleum, cattle, citrus, and other like businesses. Some have proved to be fine opportunities, if you need an initial loss for tax purposes, but many are traps. Chapter 14, "The Leaky Tax Shelters," shows how to separate valid investments from others which are mere promotions.

Chapter 15 sums up the essence of the book.

Chapter 1

THE COLLAPSE OF
THE GROWTH-STOCK BALLOON

It was unusually warm for March. The restaurant had turned on air conditioning. Seventy financial analysts jingled ice in their highball glasses as waiters put luncheon dishes on the tables. The speaker—a president of a large corporation—leaned against the wall and took a long pull at a bourbon and water.

"Look at these men," he said to me. "They've come to hear me talk about our company. They expect me to say that we will continue growing at the 15 percent annual average past rate into an indefinite future. If we did that the company would be bigger than the whole Gross National Product in another five years. Obviously we can't and just as obviously this growth madness among investors has to meet with disappointment."

His remark was prophetic. Within two years, the company had stopped "growing" at a pace which soon would have made it bigger than the national economy. And the whole idea of "growth" as an investment criterion had gone bust.

It was 1969 when the sky started falling, and by 1970, high stock prices had dropped on the unsophisticated heads of 30.8 million small investors. Conglomerates, computer companies, makers of mobile homes, and other ornaments of the former bull market's blue yonder fell fast. Even banks, mutual funds, and pension trusts had become aware that something more serious was going on than in 1962 or 1966.

Average stock prices, as measured by the broad New York Stock Exchange Index which covers all listed issues on the Big Board, declined a total of 39½ percent from the high in late 1968 to the May, 1970, low. The narrower Dow Jones Industrial Average, embracing only thirty stocks, dropped less (36 percent) because of its blue-chip makeup. Measured by either the 36 percent decline in the DJIA or the 39½ percent drop of the NYSE Index, the bear market was the longest since the depression-filled thirties and the deepest in extent of decline.

Devastating losses of capital value beset holders of "growth" stocks that analysts and their flocks had alike believed could only go up. Some of the losses were staggering.

For Freeport Minerals 1967 had been a good year. Freeport's earnings came to $2.49 per share and stood atop a five-year trend of rising earnings. The stock sold for 78; some lucky stockholders had purchased it as low as 9 five years before. Then earnings stumbled. So did the price. The stockholders who held Freeport at 78 in 1967 saw it sell as low as 11 in 1970.

For nine years, profits of Foremost-McKesson, Inc. rose steadily. Stockholders of the drug firm watched the stock shoot up to 39 at the peak of the bull market in 1968. Then the stock turned down. It sold as low as 16 in the trough of the bear market.

For a long time, Russ Togs, maker of medium-priced women's wear, was a darling of investors of both sexes. Backed by steady growth in earnings, the stock stood at 48 at the height of the bull madness in 1968. It was purchasable at 9 in 1970.

International Business Machines—more a religion than a stock —hit 375 at the 1968 bull frenzy's peak. It saw 218 at the 1970 bottom.

The list can be extended, covering everything to which a "growth" label had been attached. One executive caught up in a downward spiral of stock prices told me: "Now I know what investment people mean when they say that nothing is deader than a busted fad. Growth stocks are dead."

It is doubtful that a generation of average investors will ever again take up a concept which has cost them so dearly in lost capital and lessened self-esteem. If the late Bernard Baruch had been around for the growth-stock ding-dong, he might have told them that fads and mass delusions are no new things either in Wall Street or in the rest of mankind's group activities. One of his favorite sayings was: "Whenever I see a new madness taking hold, I remind myself that two and two still equal four and always will."

Milton Friedman, a noted economist, put it differently: "The whole science of economics," he stated, "can be summed up in five words: 'There is no free lunch.'"

The average investor did not heed such words. Nor did he listen to cautious analysts—there were a few even in the frenzied late years of the sixties—who warned that growth does not go on forever; it occurs in phases. There are phases in a corporation's existence when all conditions are right and earnings grow fat from one year to another, fatter still the third and fourth years. Sometimes these phases go on for a decade or longer. That is what fooled so many investors into thinking that growth would continue forever.

Another factor that the average investor was not aware of was that the earnings of many (not all) apparently growing companies had not grown at all but had been made to appear to expand by judicious (and sometimes culpable) accounting methods. Partly, the debacles of so many corporations were due to what one analyst termed chain letter earnings. Companies had marked up their income statements as merchants mark up sweaters and blouses. Alan Abelson, respected managing editor of the national business publication, *Barron's*, described such a setup in commenting (*Barron's*, Aug. 17, 1970) upon the annual report of a favorite growth-concept company:

> Once you get past the cover and the "highlights table" showing how fast everything at Telex is going up, the annual is fairly standard fare. The usual cheery message to stockholders, photographs of the top officers all looking dignified, the inevitable pictures of electronic devices all looking sophisticated. Not until we reached the fine print under the heading "Notes to Consolidated Financial Statements" did we find anything really noteworthy.

In particular, we suggest heading straight for Note 2, entitled "Leases and sales of computer peripheral equipment." Not only is it the longest of the footnotes, but it is also perhaps the most thought-provoking. The most interesting part deals with the way Telex accounts for the income received for its leased computer peripheral equipment. (Telex, we might interject here, is an electronics firm which, among other things, makes digital tape drives and disk drives.) Note 2 states: "For the greatest majority of the company's leases, the minimum guaranteed period is one year. For such leases, the transactions have been accounted for as sales for the full price of the equipment upon delivery." What this means simply is that by treating these leases—most of which may be canceled after one year—as a sale, Telex is able to report as current profits money which it may not earn for up to five years. The risk, of course, is that technological change, not unknown in data processing, may obsolete the equipment before the lease is able to yield what the company assumes it will.

Some conglomerates went farther than this. Operating in widely spaced fields, they tended to buy out or merge with any kind of firm they could acquire. One leading conglomerate was in movie-making, lead mining, automobile parts, industrial supplies, paper and forest products, technological systems, metal forms, chemicals, and consumer goods. The divisions of another leading conglomerate included hotels, telephone and communications utilities, electronic equipment manufacture, consumer services, insurance, and real estate. A third comprised shipyards, sophisticated electronics, business systems, metal-processing, foods, transportation, ocean shipping, aircraft machine overhaul, and recreation—in addition to miscellaneous smaller divisions.

"Who can be expert in all of those areas?" wondered one commentator.

The conglomerators proved expert in accounting procedures, however. On May 1, 1970, I commented in the weekly Markstein Letter on creditability of published figures about corporations' earnings:

Most investment analysis is based upon study of earnings, profits, sales, and the trends of these. Much has happened to shade the believability of published figures. Some things in this America of ours are supposed to be above suspicion. Until recently, we believed that if you saw a thing written down on white paper with black ink it was to be taken at face value, particularly if it happened to be a set of numbers arranged in journals and ledgers and most especially if it bore the sacred stamp of a Certified Public Accountant.

Most observers didn't notice that the CPA was only certifying that the books were accurate as far as they went and that they seemed to have been kept on a basis consistent with other years. The management, the CPA was saying, hadn't falsified anything or put part of its inventory down at double actual cost. The CPA didn't say much more than that.

Most corporations' books were and are straight. But a few are based upon scrambled methodology and occasionally upon concepts that the accounting profession's policy-making Accounting Principles Board is increasingly finding to be unacceptable.

When the books describe a corporation's sales volume, they are scrupulously honest. But sales volume is not an important statistic in reaching valid investment decisions. Neither (unless generation of current income is your objective) is the amount paid out for dividends. But you can't always believe, and in many cases cannot compare, figures relating to per-share earnings.

Non-accountants are surprised to learn that the books can say almost anything management wants them to say. Accounting is not an exact science. Its critics say it isn't a science at all. Some of the more bitter critics say it isn't even an art. In the hands of some people, bookkeeping has become a trap. But a legal one.

The trick is not what is entered on a corporation's books, but how. In 1969, the stocks of wide-ranging conglomerate corporations that controlled operations as far-spread as movies and mining, auto trailers and automatic typewriters, came a cropper. Investors suddenly discovered something that thoughtful analysts had known all along and that many of the analysts had repeatedly proclaimed to an unheeding Wall Street. Companies' books didn't always present a consistent picture of operations at all. Although many of the conglomerates were solid operating entities, as respectable as your Aunt Sallie, they were tarred with the brush that splattered suspicion on all conglomerate earnings.

Conglomerates grew because their earnings grew. The earnings, in turn, made higher stock prices. The higher stock prices gave conglomerators necessary Chinese Money to buy up still more unrelated corporations and start the process going again.

There are many ways to make earnings grow at a pencil stroke. Depreciation periods can be lengthened out. Expenses that most corporations charge off as incurred are sometimes put on a long-time depreciation table to lessen the cost bite, hence increase the earnings, for a current year. It was pointed out by one observer that with two giants in a growing field (neither a conglomerate and both conservatively managed), one consolidated all profits of its foreign subsidiaries so that these appeared as part of the parent company's earnings. The other brought into earnings only the dividends actually received from foreign subsidiaries. Had Company A kept books as did Company B, its earnings would have tripled. Had Company B kept books in the manner of Company A, earnings would have been non-existent.

These accounting methods need an endless supply of new takeovers to keep earnings "growing" because changes such as lengthened depreciation can be worked only once. Conglomerate acquisitions for increased earnings called for endless takeovers and this proved impossible. When the takeovers slowed, so did earnings growth.

Beginning in 1968, the Accounting Principles Board bore down on its professional members to disallow more flagrant entry-type earnings. Takeovers became harder to consummate as the bear market forced down prices of stock on which conglomerates depended for takeover bid currency.

Inflation, which began to get out of hand in 1967 and has raged ever since, played its part in the death of the corporate growth concept. At first inflation appeared to produce good effects; it seemed logical that stocks' earnings and therefore their prices continue to expand with the contraction of the dollar. But inflation's effects soon veered from good to bad. It became an evil in itself. Every increase tended to ripple out through the economy.

In 1969 and 1970, increasing numbers of consumers were saying in family conferences: "Things cost too much. We'll have to retrench." When consumers retrenched, merchandise stayed on retailers' shelves, retailers did not re-order from distributors, distributors' orders at the factory level decreased, and inflation, which many had considered the ingredient for growth, became a cause of profit stagnation instead.

Battered by accounting creditability gaps, inflation, and unwillingness to pay for earnings ten or twenty years off, the growth concept staggered on. It continued a factor in determining stock prices until the coup de grâce came from non-liquidity. On June 26, 1970, I wrote to Markstein Letter clients:

> One of the frightening things in the present economic picture is the grinding poverty of big corporations. They can meet their payrolls. Most can finance day to day business operation. But they are as poor as church mice . . . when it comes to sizable sums. Witness the petition for reorganization under bankruptcy laws filed by Penn Central when a big bailout package of money guarantees wasn't obtained from Washington.
>
> Only 24 months ago some analysts were proclaiming that the Penn Central was going to be the greatest transportation company ever seen. It would, they said, possibly blossom into the biggest, best-run real estate firm on record. And now in a short time, this "biggest," "best" firm is in bankruptcy. If this can befall the big, what of the small companies?
>
> Penn Central is not the only example of the frightening lack of liquidity in the American business community. A subsidiary of giant American Telephone paid 9.35 percent on a bond issue. Lockheed is in dire money straits.

Smaller corporations sometimes go to the wall. Only a
trickle of trouble is seeping through the cracked financial
dikes so far. More and worse may be ahead.

Within two months after that warning had been written, some
growth corporations, pressed for operating funds, were paying
bills in sixty to ninety days. Sometimes, orders which were
counted upon for continuance of earnings growth had to be
cancelled because pinched customers couldn't find the means
with which to buy. McDonnell-Douglas revealed that "as a result
of financial problems several airline customers have experienced
difficulty in arranging financing to take delivery of completed
aircraft, in making progress payments on time, or in meeting
current installments of principal and interest in connection with
aircraft financing."

In the growth field of computer manufacture, a large company
regretfully accepted cancellation of a $60 million order—the
single largest computer order ever placed—because financing
could not be arranged.

Many of the Wall Street firms which had underwritten, sold,
recommended, and reveled in growth stocks were also on the
critical lists. Paraphrasing General MacArthur's remark about old
soldiers, a Wall Street wag remarked that old brokerage firms
don't die, they merge. Such familiar names as F. I. duPont and
Glore, Forgan became a single firm. Prestigious Blair and Co.
closed branch offices that once numbered 38 from coast to coast.
Dempsey-Tegeler, an old-line, respected name, went into liquidation because of what New York Stock Exchange officials called
operational and financial problems. Others declared bankruptcy
or vanished into the merger mill.

A nut fringe of analysts who picked growth stocks by zodiac,
sunspots, and waves of varying kinds hadn't helped to make the
growth concept respectable during its late days. As the concept
died, so did the number of occult prognosticators. "No loss there
at any rate," remarked an official of the professional Financial
Analysts Federation. "But I regret the going of the growth madness. It was fun—and sometimes profitable."

All the tricks weren't the fault of corporations or prognosticators. Sometimes the average investor lost a toe or a foot in traps
set in Wall Street itself, mutual-funds men who—sometimes in-

advertently, often deliberately—played the growth concept as a numbers game.

The regular securities that investors buy on exchanges or over the counter are registered with the Securities and Exchange Commission. Unregistered letter stocks are not. These stocks come into existence when a company needs capital and does not want to go through the SEC's regulatory process. The company can sell stock to big buyers who sign letters of investment intent promising to hold the letter stock for a specified length of time— usually two years—without distributing it to the public. The then popular go-go funds snapped up such stocks because they could buy at one-fourth to one-third discounts and then mark the stock up to secure quick performance on their books.

"Sometimes we'd buy in the morning and have a 50 percent profit by afternoon," one ex-mutual-fund management man explained.

Then redemptions of mutual funds set in. These were partially triggered by troubles in Mates Investment Fund, a mutual which placed what proved an unreasonable percentage of its assets in letter stock of an ailing corporation. Redemptions had to be suspended until Mates could be placed on a liquid basis. When the fund resumed redemptions, shareowners found that they could realize only a fraction of the value they had believed was in their Mates holding.

Other funds experienced similar trouble. When blocks of restricted stocks had to be sold, they could be peddled only to other institutions willing to assume the bought-for-long-term investment status, and willing to face the chore of going through registration at the end of the holding period. The result was that blocks of restricted stock, purchased at a discount, had to be peddled at a further, and frequently sizable, discount.

Commented the SEC (Releases Nos. 34–8836/IA–258):

> . . . During 1968 and contrary to his representations to stockholders, Mates caused Mates Investment Fund, Inc., a registered investment company, to invest substantial sums in "restricted securities" which could not be publicly sold without prior registration under the Securities Act. Mates, who was then president and director of Fund and dominated its investment policies, also caused the

restricted securities to be valued improperly by assigning
them values equal to the market prices of the unrestricted
securities of the same class or at a small fixed dollar discount from such market prices. The valuation methods
gave Fund, whose publicity stressed "performance," the
appearance of a greater appreciation in value than was
justified and affected investors' decisions to redeem or to
continue to hold their shares. . . . When the Fund
needed to dispose of portfolio assets to meet further redemptions and to pay bank loans obtained to purchase
restricted securities, Fund was forced to sell some of its
restricted securities at prices substantially lower than the
valuations given them by Mates and at substantial discounts from the market value of unrestricted securities of
the same class.

The Securities and Exchange Commission, moving to close the
barn door after investors' horses had broken out, now has set
rules for how letter stocks are valued in arriving at mutual-fund
net-asset values. Previously the method of valuation depended
upon the conscience of the fund manager. The SEC also set
bounds on the amount of letter stock a fund might hold. By that
time the question had become academic. Losses were so large
and shareowner disillusionment so profound that few mutual
managers would again risk burned fingers with restricted investments.

Other mutuals went for the hedge concept. This theory of investing called for a fund to carry both "long" and "short" positions, owning some stocks and selling others short. The idea was
that by hedging, a fund would benefit from both up and down
movements and, by adjusting the percentages of longs and shorts
it could nullify—even gain from—bear markets. Most hedge
funds are private partnerships and, although many had disastrous
losses in the big downturn, some fared well. Not so publicly-
owned mutual funds which followed the hedging plan. According to a listing of four-year performance results among funds
which aimed to produce capital gains for their shareowners, the
worst performances were turned in by two hedge operations. One
lost 65.7 percent of investors' capital in a period when the market
dropped only half as much.

Investors' disenchantment with mutual funds—not always justified since some did well in a difficult time—had serious results for the overall market. In May, 1971, for the first time in history, the funds had greater redemptions than sales. This occurred again in June and July. In August things picked up.

Stock markets were, and for a long time had been, dominated by institutions. The mutual funds, it is true, are only one kind of institution. There are also insurance companies, pension funds, and banks' trust departments. Mutual funds, while not the largest of these groups, are conceivably the most important in setting stock prices. They hold greater percentages of common stocks in their portfolios than do other institutions, which also go in for bonds, investment in mortgages, and even land. Moreover, it is the mutual funds which swing and rock in the market, turning over their portfolios constantly. *Thus it is probably the mutual funds' buying of stocks that accounts for the fact that 39 percent of the listed stocks are turned over enough to create 70 percent of the trading activity.*

In 1929, it was the dumping of stocks margined as little as 10 percent which created the massive selling waves that carried prices down to disaster level and induced so many to end it all by a plunge out of the window while their stocks were plunging on the board.

Suppose that this trend of redemptions exceeding sales in the mutual-fund industry were to continue and accelerate. The funds do not keep vast sums of cash on hand for redemption. They could be forced to sell stocks in order to raise money to meet redemptions. That would force down prices of the stocks they hold, building at least a minor panic which, in turn, could trigger additional redemption demands *which would start the process going again in exactly the way 10 percent margins triggered disaster back in 1929.*

Wall Street advisers, the bear market revealed, were sometimes less than perceptive in understanding forces below the surface. Few foresaw the bear trouble before it was upon them in full force. Few advised retrenching by outright sale of securities until sunny skies should reappear. Almost none avoided the growth madness and the craze for mutual-fund performance.

Succeeding chapters will detail some sensible solutions to the problem of investing in a new day when growth has become a dirty word and when hard realities govern investment values.

The hardest reality for traditionally minded investors to accept is that social and ecological goals that are not directly related to growth and profits are going to play a major role in the investment scene. It's not just that certain types of stock or investment methods have been shown to be risky bets, but that the whole concept of unlimited and undirected economic growth has come into question.

In the years after World War II, America developed the greatest technology ever seen. Jobs were created, factories proliferated, a throw-away consciousness evolved in which not only beer and soft drink bottles but medical equipment, automobiles, even people, were considered objects to be used up and discarded.

Times were prosperous but problems were increasing. In building factories and extending city suburbs we had destroyed the room for living which gave a reason to the drive for prosperity.

Moreover, the by-products of prosperity, particularly industrial pollution, began to be seen as major threats to everyone's well-being. It was good business but not necessarily good living. And now it's not even necessarily good business. Companies that fail to regulate themselves can expect sooner or later to have regulations forced upon them.

The seventies and eighties will be different from the fifties and sixties. Concentration on growth per se is over. Emphasis will be on more meaningful living, as measured in things other than bank balances and gaudy cars.

The criterion is whether a new product or method will increase the total of human good rather than whom it will benefit and to what degree. The belief has grown that corporations exist to serve humanity and not make black-ink entries on the bottom line of a profit and loss statement. You may not agree with the new attitude. But you have to recognize it if you are to benefit in a new world which rejects growth and most of the materialism for which it stood. Two keys, then, to successful choice of investment vehicles in the years ahead are ecology and the service of social ends, even to the temporary exclusion of immediate profits.

Chapter 2

POSTULATING A BUSINESS
CLIMATE FOR INVESTMENT

The immediate economic background is not a positive one. It calls for continuing inflation and dollar troubles. Controls over the economy and individual lives are likely to remain but not work well. A depression is possible. But afterward the outlook becomes better—bright, in fact. Investment with that in view is likely to make investors rich before 1980 rolls around.

INFLATION WON'T STOP

Inflation begins with more money chasing the same goods. This condition began to be operative in the sixties when the Federal Reserve expanded money supply at a frighteningly fast rate. The average rate of increase during post-World War II years was about 2.5 percent. This kept pace with increase in productivity. Far faster than productivity increases, however, were the later swollen 6 percent money stock increases.

The Federal Reserve in 1969 stopped money-supply growth. Predictably, the economy began to turn over like a dying whale as recession took hold. Alarmed, the Federal Reserve in early 1970 was compelled to restore growth of money supply. Meanwhile, prices tended to increase even faster. This occurred because a second cause of inflation had taken over—cost-push inflation.

It works this way: A manufacturer's costs go up. So he raises the price of his merchandise by a small percentage and ships it to the wholesaler. The truck line which carries the goods must pay higher wages. It, too, raises the tab for carrying the goods to the distributor. He raises his prices accordingly. And in order not to be swamped under the increases, he is forced to add a normal markup to the increases themselves. Then he ships to the retail store. Again the cost of transportation is higher, so that there is a series of increases on the cost by the time this merchandise reaches the retailer. He, too, is compelled to add his regular markup percentage to the increases themselves as well as to the old base price. He also may add a further increase he is not compelled to have. When the merchandise reaches the consumer, the price has been upped a great deal. Inflation feeds on itself.

In August, 1971, President Richard M. Nixon proposed actions designed to control inflation. These included wage and price controls along with a surcharge on imported goods and other steps designed to control the nation's monetary ills, many caused by inflation. Wags dubbed the program "Nixonomics."

The case against Phases One or Two—or succeeding stages of the anti-inflation effort—being successful in putting a stop to inroads of the inflationary dragon was put by the First National City Bank of New York's *Monthly Economic Letter*, October, 1971:

> The initial feeling of relief that—rightly or wrongly— greeted the President's new economic program has given way to hard questions about its ultimate impact. Crucial among them is whether a program that is designed half to stimulate output through fiscal measures and half to contain price pressures through market intervention can long survive.
>
> . . . Despite a large body of evidence that similar programs have failed in the past, [the Administration] is attempting to pump up aggregate demand while containing price pressures through an incomes policy.

. . . Implicit in the anti-inflation policy the Administration is now espousing is the "devil" theory of inflation. Primary responsibility for inflation is said to rest on those industries where wages and prices are rising more than they "ought" to—and the culprits can be identified. All that is needed is a practical formula to tell how prices and wages ought to behave. With such a formula, presumably it would be known whenever a union, firm or industry was exercising "excessive market power" . . . Empirical evidence supports the view that output per man-hour ultimately is the main determinant of the trend of real wages and that an industry's productivity trend also influences its relative price behavior. But whether the economic truth embodied in productivity guidelines renders them of practical value is another question. Guidelines of the sort set up by the Kennedy Administration and in European countries did not prevent or even seriously limit price inflation. Nor would the existence of special bipartite or tripartite machinery promise to affect the results in any systematic way. Arthur Ross, a former Commissioner of Labor Statistics, in his study of wage-price guidelines, concluded that "two of the European countries with the most elaborate organization for incomes policy have been the Netherlands and the United Kingdom." But, "they had the highest labor cost indexes and were in the upper half in terms of the consumer price indexes" of all the countries in Europe with the exception of France.

An American administration faced with recession or any kind of developing economic troubles must take steps to avert them if it wants to be returned to office in the next election. That means at such times the pursuit of easy money policies; these compel an administration to abandon no-growth monetary policies as soon as the shoe begins to pinch voters' incomes seriously.

The result of the probable failure of controls over wages and prices and of the realities of office which compel money stimulation when troubled times loom on the horizon is that inflation cannot be expected to stop. It might be rendered quiescent from time to time. But the fires of rising prices and dwindling dollar value will break out again. They are a fact of life which must be taken into account before making investment decisions. Many believe that inflation is a bullish factor. It is not. Its effects are great in the beginning, decreasingly so in the middle stages, and positively disastrous toward the end. Corporate profits in the later stages of inflation seldom keep pace with corporations' costs of doing business. The result can be chaos compounded by bankruptcy.

SOME CONTROLS WILL STAY

Controls over the economy are popular, even when unworkable. Everybody is for some controls, usually over the other guy. Labor likes to see prices kept under a lid. Business plumps for a freeze on the wages it must pay, so that the item of labor cost it cannot control through bargaining will be controlled by the stronger force of government. The large middle group and all professional people like controls over both wages and prices in the hope of stopping a steady lessening in the purchasing power of their income dollars.

Controls can be expected to continue in force in some degree. They cannot be expected to work effectively. But they can be expected to hobble industry and commerce, make labor groups periodically angry, and create both sporadic and continuing scarcities of products.

Scarcities are the inevitable and unvarying result of controls. They must be considered as part of the background of an era in which a greater or lesser degree of control is expected to stay on the economy. When the cost, but not the price, of a product increases, it is no longer profitable to make the product. The manufacturer then makes a new product or offers a new service on which his realistic cost, not an historical record inapplicable under existing conditions, applies to the setting of a ceiling price. Soon competitors, too, turn away from the field. Result: scarcity. And for investors, threats to corporate profits and stock prices.

Scarcities can arise with suddenness and upset manufacturers' supplies as well as emptying the shelves from which consumers shop. In the period of continuing controls they are likely to be an ephemeral—and at times important—factor in the business-investment picture.

Denmark enjoyed frozen prices. The experience was so bad that after a trial period the freeze was de-iced, to be replaced with one of "friendly persuasion." It was soon found that friendly persuasion was either so amicable as to be unworkable, or else so steely that the difference between friendly and legal controls was one of semantics. Controls and their problems lingered on.

Controls sometimes become farcical. Shortly after imposition of the August, 1971, freeze, federal regulators pounced upon a hotel in Detroit: the price of pay toilets in public rest rooms had been raised. The raise was promptly rescinded and people of the Michigan metropolis were saved from the pay toilet inflation.

In another instance investment counselors—those professional advisers who guide the destinies of mutual funds and other institutional investors—were sternly prohibited from raising fees by a Securities and Exchange Commission directive, which stated:

1) The wage-price freeze is applicable to any revisions of existing contracts with respect to advisory fees which would result in increased payments to an investment adviser.

2) The percentage of net assets, whether or not based on performance related to an index, used for computing the amount of the advisory fee owned by registered investment companies to investment advisers may not lawfully be increased. This would include changes in any of the percentages involved in the computation of performance, base and minimum fees.

3) If the investment company has mailed its proxy material to its shareholders to approve an increase in the advisory fee, it may obtain the shareholders' vote but may not put any increase into effect during the period of the wage-price freeze.

One adviser commented: "That probably saved the average investor a dollar and a half yearly."

Experienced financial observers felt during late 1971 that the freeze was nevertheless likely to linger over the United States.

CONTINUING DOLLAR TROUBLES

Inflation makes American goods cost more in relation to goods from lands less troubled with erosion of their currency or possessed of more efficient labor forces. Controls and freezes dwindle the supply of some goods sometimes—often unexpectedly.

Until August, 1971, international trade was carried on under a gold exchange standard. Other currencies were convertible into U.S. dollars. These in turn were exchangeable (by central banks, not by you or me) into gold. Then came the announcement of suspension of dollar redemption for gold.

After that, prices of other money, formerly pegged to set numbers of dollars—the Canadian dollar and German mark had been exceptions—all "floated" with no fixed rates of exchange upon which a trader might count from one month to another. This might seem to have little relationship to the process of investing in the United States in the troubled decade of the seventies. It has a great deal of relevance, however. How American inflationary troubles that triggered the crisis of 1971 will lead to other crises unless inflation is controlled, was explained in the October, 1971, *Monthly Economic Letter* of the First National City Bank:

> With his customary prescience, Irving Fisher described the origin of the world's dollar problem years ago:
>
> ". . . no great increase of money (M) in any one country or locality can occur (he said) without spreading to other countries or localities. As soon as local prices have risen enough to make it profitable to sell at the high prices in that place and buy at the low prices elsewhere, money will be exported. The production of gold in Colorado and Alaska first results in higher prices in Colorado and Alaska, then in sending gold to other sections of the United States, then in higher prices throughout the United States, then in export abroad, and finally in higher prices throughout the gold-using world."
>
> It is not difficult to recognize features of the old gold standard in today's international payments system. But the dollar now serves the role formerly played by gold.

Much of the sales, profit, and future potential of American industry in an increasingly one-world atmosphere lay in its participation (in some cases near dominance) of international selling. That in turn depended upon stable and known exchange rates; without such stability a distributor in, say, Frankfurt, cannot place an order for delivery in six months since he does not know how many marks he will have to put up at that time to meet the dollar price of the contract. Trading machinery breaks down.

In conferences aimed at reestablishing monetary order, other nations have taken the attitude that the United States should raise the price of gold, thus devaluing the existing dollar, and put its house in order. U.S. negotiators took the attitude that Europeans should themselves devalue dollars by raising the prices of their currencies relative to American money.

The problem continued and is not likely to be solved soon, despite interim stopgap arrangements. It will possibly continue for a lengthy period to be a trouble spot and a source of explosive crises, leading to more interim measures and inevitably to more crises. Uncertainty can hurt the stock market.

NEW, NEW ECONOMICS GROWS OLD

In the latter part of the 1960's, more and more attention was given to the theories of the New, New Economists led by Milton Friedman of the University of Chicago. Their thesis, briefly stated, was that the supply of money is the chief factor in the economy. If the Federal Reserve System makes more money available, factories boom, deserts bloom, and stock markets zoom. Eventually the process leads to inflation. Therefore, from time to time government planners should choke off a little of the boom, bloom, and zoom by lessening the flow of dollars through the Federal Reserve's monetary hoses.

This monetarist philosophy differed from that of the Old, New Economists, who hold to the theories of John Maynard Lord Keynes, British speculator and economist, who had taught that both monetary and fiscal steps (including the balancing and unbalancing of government budgets) are needed to regulate the economy.

In 1968, Keynesian fiscal steps were taken to control inflation without decreasing money supply. Inflation sailed on. "Aha!" crowed the New, New Economists. "Their system doesn't work. Now we will try ours."

In 1969 and 1970, their brand of true belief was in. Money supply was decreased. Promptly, as specified, the economy turned over and began to die. Soon recession ensued. However, inflation still sailed on.

Worried, the New, New men, who by now were in command, began to pump more money into the economy. Money-supply increases became the highest in recorded memory.

Recession, however, proved resistant. It worsened instead of getting better. And inflation became rampant. "As I shopped in the supermarket one morning, I saw a marker with a clicking machine in his hand around the corner from the ice cream, by the canned peas," one housewife reported in the summer of 1971. "He was adding to the price of everything. I raced him all the way past the meats and into the housewares, finally to the check-out, buying before he could up prices by 10 percent."

By the fall of the same year this housewife sadly reported that she didn't bother to race any longer. "Recession is so bad I can't afford anything but necessities any longer."

The Chicago School of Economics is in lessened favor. As a factor in making investment decisions, its pronouncements and policies are not to be reckoned in determining the investment climate of the coming decade.

That climate offers both bright and dark prospects.

DEPRESSION?

In November, 1971, I suggested to two business magazine editors an article on the probability of a coming depression. Their replies were enlightening.

"No use talking about the coming depression to our readers," one editor told me. "They've got it now. So have we."

The other editor said:

"You're right, Dave. It's depression. So much so that I can only pay you two-thirds the former price for the article. Is this agreeable?" (It wasn't.)

The 1929–1933 Depression left scars on America and the rest of the world and an abiding conviction that no such calamity must ever be allowed to happen again. Toward that end, a number of social and money-management statutes were passed, and men breathed easier. "Except for minor ups and downs, the economic cycle has been abolished," they told themselves. In 1970 and 1971, as unemployment mounted almost as fast as prices and factory production dropped, the extent of the picture was partially hidden by statistics with which Washington continually tinkered to make black seem, if not white, gray. The United States was plunging into something more serious than anything since the thirties. A generation unused to anything except ever-mounting prosperity couldn't believe it.

"Nixonomics" in 1971 called for, among other things, imposition of higher import duties on many foreign goods. The aim was to increase the salability of U.S.-made products. The effect was to provoke retaliation and worsening unemployment in countries that had depended upon sales in the wide American market.

Writing in the *Business Review* of the Federal Reserve Bank of Dallas, October, 1971, Philip E. Coldwell, president of that bank, noted:

> . . . The causal factors of our economic and financial problems of today have roots which go back many years, but I shall attempt to limit my discussion to their recent impact. No special priorities are implied by the order in which these factors are presented.
>
> One good starting point seems to be the familiar business cycle, for in a relatively free enterprise system there are multitudes of decisions which, if suddenly made in a concerted direction, can shift the balance of the economy and require strong offsetting actions to maintain stability. Over the past five years, we have witnessed just such a change, as Government sought to finance an underestimated war cost without compensating taxes. This cost was superimposed on an economy growing at a remarkable rate, with the not unusual result of creating heavy inflationary pressures. Businessmen began the all-too-familiar mass decision-making process of overextending

capital investment, hoarding labor, and building inventories. These added fire to the brightly glowing boom and turned it into an incipient inferno of inflation.

. . . If our inherent system problems were the only ones causing our present crisis, we could act with confidence that recovery in a sustainable, generally noninflationary environment could be achieved. Unfortunately, there are other matters which seem to have changed the underlying responses of the economy. Some of these changes have been the growing concentration of business, the development of conglomerates and multinational corporate concepts, and the heavy debt structures created to finance such ventures. The high degree of corporate financing expertise and the leverage employed almost assured problems if the rate of growth in the economy ever slowed. In a way, this development was a part of the excesses of speculation normally seen at boom times, but the concentration also reflected a structural shift which national stabilization policies were not adjusted to nor policy-makers equipped to handle.

. . . As industry concentrated, so did union power. And with this power, a steady diet of rising wages and costs fueled the price increase efforts of business, which further stimulated the large capital goods boom and brought faster introduction of laborsaving devices. The high cost of doing business domestically turned more business eyes on foreign fields, where labor costs were more moderate.

This chain of events was reinforced by another shift in American life which had been underway since the thirties—to increased welfare, Social Security, retirement, and fringe benefits. These and other social efforts, including the newer ones in ecology and pollution, brought business costs to a critical level and further supported business decisions to raise prices and to produce abroad for export to the U.S. market. These trends converged in the late 1960's, causing a massive increase in imports, a growing lack of competitiveness for U.S. exports, and a serious acceleration of the deterioration in our balance of payments.

AFTER DEPRESSION—BOOM

A new boom may be the central fact for successful investing in our decade. It should start no later than the middle of the 1970's, after depression has swept out the inefficiencies of the earlier bust and after things in manufacturing, selling and service industries have had the accumulated fat of twenty years boiled away. The records of man's commercial history show that not only do fat times always succeed lean days, but that the good eras can be expected to last two to four times as long.

I believe that after a short period in the desert, we're going to emerge into a land of milk and honey. With boom can come a steady climb in stock prices, fueled not only by the rising earnings for the years after 1975, but also by demand from billion-dollar investors hungry for stocks. The "institutions"—insurance companies, bank trust departments, and so on—will be bidding increasingly for a supply of stocks expected to rise less rapidly than the increase in money bidding to buy the shares.

A New York Stock Exchange research study published in January, 1970, showed that:

(1) Nonprofit institutions which owned $1.5 billion in stocks in 1968 and $3.0 billion in 1970 would hold an estimated $4.0 billion by 1980.

(2) Life insurance companies possessed $1.3 billion in stocks in 1968 and $3.9 by 1970. They would hold, the NYSE estimate showed, $5.5 billion by 1980.

(3) Noninsured private pension funds, with $6.1 billion in stocks in 1968 and $11.1 billion in 1970, would have increased their holdings to $13.3 billion at the close of the decade.

(4) Open-end investment companies would increase stock holdings 2.2 times by 1980.

(5) The state and local government retirement plans, cautiously holding $600 million in stocks in 1968 and $1.2 billion by 1970, would own $1.5 billion in 1980.

(6) Mutual savings banks would increase their holdings by

50 percent at the end of the decade. (This would not be as significant as it appears, since these owned only $200 million in 1970, according to New York Stock Exchange survey statistics.)

With increased institutional dominance of the stock market can come increased instability. Institutions have proved themselves to be weathervane investors, frequently following each others' leads and guided in many cases by computer printouts which show a dozen different managers the same buy or sell signals at the same time, so that their simultaneous buying and selling creates sudden price surges followed by sudden losses. The institutions which overshadow individual investors at present, and will to a greater degree in future markets, have not been the steadying influence which their size and presumably staid professional management would have led the average investor to expect.

CERTAIN CORPORATIONS WILL PROSPER IN THIS CLIMATE

In the early and middle 1960's, it was the corporation intent upon technological change which made the headlines and the most active stock lists. Then technology faded as a force to motivate higher stock prices. Technical men often proved duds at the very different game of producing corporate profits. In their place as investor favorites stepped the conglomerators.

These men promised to take a number of parts in the form of smaller companies and put them together into a whole which would be greater than the sum of the parts. They had a name for this hopeful process. They called it *synergism*. In some cases, as investors and analysts later learned, synergism was accomplished by means of rigged books and doubtful accounting methods.

Into the places of the conglomerators and the places earlier vacated by technologists who promised the moon and delivered it, but neglected to also deliver corporate net profits along the way, will step corporations and managements in these areas:

(1) Companies, regardless of their fields or the products they make, which are in tune with the "in" philosophy that making

profits isn't all a corporation is about. It must likewise exist to serve a social need. Paradoxically, it is in the serving of social needs that profits may best be picked up—because these needs *must* be met in the coming decades.

(2) Service industries; these are going to be proportionally more important than manufacturing industries.

(3) In addition to serving social aims, the successful corporations will be those that respond to our troubled world. Our cities are blighted and companies which unblight them should prosper. So should investors in stocks of such companies. Our streets are crime-ridden and our homes unsafe. Crime control companies can be in the front of any list of profitable investment media. The clogged streets and freeways must be unjammed if workers are not to spend more hours getting to and from places of work than toiling at their desks and machines. Rapid transit is the only workable answer. Companies that come up with imaginative ways to provide this can pay their investors well.

(4) Imagination and creativity will continue to pay off in any field.

Chapter 3

NEW APPROACHES TO
STOCK VALUATION

The techniques of investing, like those of professional football, change as years and coaches' tinkering make a Notre Dame box or a single wing obsolete, and as new formations and methods come into use. The growth technique of investing is out. Reliance upon earnings figures has gone the way of pass-punt-and-pray as a system for winning gridiron encounters. The power "I" and the wishbone T have taken the place of the single wing. Different techniques are needed now in investing as well.

THE BALANCE SHEET RIDES AGAIN

Pick up an annual report to stockholders from any corporation and you will see two basic sets of figures. One is called an income statement; it is sometimes headed profit and loss statement. It details what money was taken in, the expenses incurred, and how much (if any) was left for net profit. It will probably express this both as overall profit and as net earnings per share.

The other statement is usually titled "Balance Sheet"; occasionally it is labeled a statement of assets or a statement of net worth. It lists the assets of a corporation from cash in the bank to buildings on the ground, including inventories, amounts owed to the company, and securities in its portfolio. On the other side are detailed liabilities—the sums owed long-term debtors such as bondholders, dollars due to routine creditors such as suppliers, and other things which take away from a company's owned assets. The difference between them (provided it is on the asset side) is expressed as net worth. The balance sheet shows liquid and long-term assets on which a company's ability to generate profits is ultimately based. The income statement shows what those profits are—always with the proviso that the accounting methods have not been gimmicked. (The balance sheet can also be gimmicked. Anything can. But it is not done as easily nor has it been done to such an extent as the gimmicking of the income statement).

Old-fashioned uses of the balance sheet were to determine total net worth of a company and then compare it with the total valuation at which its stock was selling. If the balance sheet showed $1 million in assets and the company's 100,000 shares of stock sold at $12, an analyst of the rolltop-desk days would say that the price of the stock was above "book value," which came to $10 per share in this case and compared to a price of $12 on the exchange where Amalgamated Buggywhip was traded.

Book value was, and to some extent still is, a useful statistic. Most companies' stocks sell above book value. When a stock is selling below book value, an interesting investment opportunity begins to become apparent.

You can take the old-fashioned concept of book value as a starting point. If book value has been well and truly expressed (it's easy to overstate value of a building for which no ready market exists or of machinery that you can't sell at need), then a company is worth more dead than alive. It begins to attract attention from operators who might buy the firm to liquidate some of its assets, pay them out to stockholders, including themselves, to reimburse the cost of obtaining control, and then operate the remaining corporate shell or else merge it into another part of the operators' empire. If that happens, you, as an outside stockholder, are all to the good. Chances are that the investment, broken up and sold off, is worth more than it cost you to get in. If that were not so, the group which brought off the breakup coup would not have bothered.

Such breakups seldom occur, however. More often a conglomerate purchases in order to acquire fresh assets to use for paper "earnings." Sometimes a shrewd manufacturer sees the misuse or nonuse of assets that could be put to work profitably and buys in to cut fat from the company and operate rather than liquidate it. You're to the good in such a case, too, because that results in what Wall Street calls a turnaround situation—and eventually higher stock prices.

Does the asset-value approach work?

In a letter-to-the-editor published in *Forbes*, Robert J. A. Irwin, Jr., vice-president of Marine Midland Banks, Inc., New York, told how "we have tested selected investment strategies involving the computer and figures for 900 publicly-traded industrial stocks over a 19-year period (1948–67). One of the strategies tested involved the investment of equal sums of money in all stocks in which the book value exceeded the market value. These selections outperformed the Standard & Poor's index of 425 industrial stocks by an average of 70 percent each year.

"Our 'loaded laggards' appreciated by 20.6 percent per year. The average increase for the S & P 425-stock index was about 12.1 percent per year and the average yearly percentage increase for the entire list was 17 percent. There were only six years out of the nineteen in which the group did not outperform the S & P stock index."

Yet people do not pay as much attention to book value as you'd expect. A reason is that liquidation of corporate assets is not always simple—few want old brick buildings in a decaying industrial area—and the assets, even if put to use, might not be useful if they are obsolete or rusted away.

People do pay attention—and you're likely to make money in the changed investment atmosphere ahead if you do this—to a figure revealed by the balance sheet which is called *quick assets*. It is not always expressed as such. You have to dig it out of many balance sheets. Quick assets consist of cash and things which are considered the equivalent of cash because they can be speedily converted into ready money. Examples are government or other high-grade bonds and securities in a company portfolio, when a good market exists on which the securities can be sold; and accounts receivable (money owed the company on current bills outstanding), provided this is truly current and owed by debtors who can be counted on to pay within routinely short periods of time.

When a corporation possesses quick assets per share above the selling price of the stock, or even equal to or slightly under market price, then a situation exists for early profits. Conglomerators, liquidators, and corporate bargain searchers are going to be attracted. Beware a seemingly good quick-assets situation, however, where the stock of the company is closely held. An example was one shipping company whose realizable quick assets were above selling price of the stock. An associate and I considered the possibilities of a syndicate buying control and distributing the quick assets, which would have given them and the other stockholders a profit well above current price of the stock while retaining intact the equipment, personnel, and long-term assets for continued operation as a shipping line. Quick-assets data can be abstracted from the balance sheet.

"Looks lovely, doesn't it?" my associate said. "But it won't work. Here's why: No group can get control. Less than 20 people own 53 percent of the corporation. All are officers and each is so steeped in the company as a way of life that he would as readily consider dismemberment of the fifty American states as he would a selloff of one of the assets that firm has accumulated in its half century of operation. Even if someone accumulated all of the floating supply on the market—an unlikely thing—and was able to do so without running up the price too much above the present attractive level, he would run into the stone wall of that intransigent group. It won't work."

My associate was right. Years afterward, when the old guard had passed and a generation of heirs proved willing to sell out for the promise of profit, the acquisition was executed by an outside group and proved profitable.

PARLAY AND PLOWBACK

If you mentioned dividends to a growth-conscious investor during the decade of the sixties, he would answer: "Those things? Who needs current income? The tax collector gets a big bite and what's left is not enough compared to the gains I can get from good-growth stocks."

"Good-growth stocks" proved a weak reed. But income can go on, provided the vehicle chosen to produce the income is chosen wisely (more on how to do this in a coming chapter).

The operative techniques are parlay and plowback.

You parlay an investment when you take the proceeds of a successful play and reinvest the whole. Say you've spotted an undervalued situation and invested $1,000 in the stock. A conglomerate bids up the shares and you sell out for $1,500, less the commissions which your friendly broker won't neglect to assess on both purchase and sale. Say you next find another interesting situation—you parlay when you put the whole $1,500 into the new investment.

This is not as risky as it might seem. If you parlay a racehorse bet and the second wager loses, you have dropped the whole bundle and would be justified in wishing you had retained at least the winnings from the first gamble. It isn't so with investing. In practice, no purchase will go 100 percent sour as does a wager on a losing horse. If the second investment fails to work out, you're likely to still have $1,200 or $1,300 after cutting the loss, while if it goes as planned you might realize $2,000 to $2,500 on the bundle.

Take plowback. You've bought a bond of high quality which yields 7 percent income a year. You can spend the income on a new car or a dinner at a good restaurant, depending upon the amount of the original investment and how much it brings in at 7 percent. Or you can carefully reinvest the proceeds in new bonds when you receive it. The first course is called fun. The latter is known as plowing back. If you plow back each dollar of interest, you may end up with an investment satisfyingly larger than the amount you started with.

FOLLOW THOSE WITH INSIDE KNOWLEDGE

You can't know what the president and other officers of a corporation think about its future, other than the sometimes biased and usually well-hedged remarks they make before gatherings of financial analysts. But you can tell what they are *doing*. That is more important.

You can get this information for a few dollars a year. Write to the Superintendent of Documents, Government Printing Office, Washington, D.C. 20402, for a subscription to *Official Summary of Security Transactions and Holdings*. It will tell you each month what corporate insiders are doing with the stocks of their companies.

An "insider" is an officer, director, or beneficial owner of 10 percent of the stock of a publicly traded company. By law all transactions in their companies' stocks must be reported to the Securities and Exchange Commission. These are then compiled and published in the *Official Summary*. No smart investors should be without it. Earnings figures may not be believable and even some balance sheet data, as noted, can be misleading at times. But when sales and purchases are made by people possessed of facts the public does not always know, these transactions become worthwhile guides.

The *Official Summary* lists names of those who bought or sold and how many shares were involved. It also defines the kind of purchase and sale. That definition helps to determine whether the transaction was routine or worth noting.

Purchases under stock option plans are generally routine. Officers of most corporations are allowed to buy company stock under the market price their stockholders pay; this is a form of compensation for their services. Purchases made under option aren't generally noteworthy as a guide to what the purchasers think of the company's future. Nor are shares received as stock dividends. If the president holds 100,000 shares and the company pays a 2 percent stock dividend, his added 2,000 shares are as routine as the two shares received by the small investor on his 100 shares. Disregard stock dividends; likewise shares received in splits. Those received by bequest or inheritance aren't valid guides either. Nor should you pay attention to stock added by exercise of rights, by gift, or in a corporate distribution.

Stock purchased in the open market, however, indicates what the insider thinks. It also indicates an opinion—although of a different sort—when the insider is selling stock in the open market to lighten his portfolio. Even this can't be considered a definite

guide to stock selection or sale unless more than one, and preferably several, officers are all doing the same thing. One man might
sell merely to diversify. Or he might cash up some shares, especially if he is an officer in the second echelon and not given a
salary of executive suite proportions. The group trend of buying
and selling is a sounder guide than actions of a single officer or
director, however highly placed. Even a group trend isn't important if there exists another trend in the other direction. Frequently three officers sell while two buy, during a month. But
when there is a clear *consensus* of buying and selling, then you've
heard something. Heed it.

In the "Personal Investing" department of *Fortune*, July, 1968,
Lawrence A. Mayer reported research on insider trading as an
investment guide. It was conducted by Shannon P. Pratt and
Charles W. DeVere of Portland (Oregon) State College. The
article noted:

> What Pratt and DeVere have done so far is to put on
> tape all insider transactions covering the period January,
> 1960, through December, 1965, for two-thirds of the com-
> panies listed on the New York Stock Exchange. (Data
> on the remaining companies are now being processed.)
> Once they had the situation taped, so to speak, Pratt and
> DeVere had the computer "buy" (or "sell") every stock
> that three or more insiders bought (or sold) in any
> given month—provided that no other insider was buck-
> ing the trend. In other words, the actions by insiders were
> considered significant only when they were unanimous.
> Only open-market transactions by insiders were used;
> exercises of options were not counted as purchases, for
> example. And only insider transactions that were re-
> ported promptly were used.
>
> . . . Assuming purchases two months after the insiders
> made theirs, stocks that were held for twelve months
> showed an average gain of 24 percent. According to the
> so-called Fisher Index, this is just about twice the aver-
> age annual return on all common stocks listed on the
> New York Stock Exchange during the period covered by
> the Portland State experiment.
>
> . . . Besides being profitable as a whole, the group of

stocks identified as buys had another considerable attraction. In studies that identify one group of stocks that outperforms another group, the high-performance group just about always contains some individual stocks that do exceptionally well but also some that are heavy losers. In the Portland State study, however, good returns were spread fairly evenly throughout the buy group, so that the degree of risk involved in actual portfolio selection was minimized.

ASSETS IN THE GROUND

The rationale behind study of assets in the ground—iron ore, oil, gold, and other natural resources including forests—as a basis for stock selection holds that while they remain in the bosom of Mother Earth, they're refrigerated for future profits. As the assets are taken out, they become priced at figures which reflect continuing inflation. Hence a company with large earthbound assets can't fail to do as well as the economy and should do better.

Like all generalizations, the theory has a hole. Labor which mines the ore, drills for the oil, or fells the trees increases in cost with inflation—often faster.

To see how well the theory functioned under a trying set of market circumstances, I examined results for 1964, 1965, 1966, 1967, 1968, and 1969. During that time the popular Dow Jones Industrial Average appreciated 5.9 percent. This was computed by taking the average of the high and low prices for 1964 and 1969. In 1964 the Dow saw a high of 891.71 and low of 766.08. The figures for 1969 were 985.85 and 769.93, respectively, giving an average price on the Dow of 828.89 in 1965 and 877.89 in 1969.

Among *Barron's* industry group averages are five which measure price progress of companies having assets in (or on) the ground. Using the same method of computation—averaging off high and low prices for the starting and ending years of the six-year period and comparing average gains and losses—the five asset-rich stock groups fared as follows:

Gold mining	Plus 141.0 percent
Nonferrous metals	Plus 93.0 percent
Oil	Plus 1.0 percent
Paper	Plus 24.4 percent
Steel and iron	(Minus 9.8 percent)

All except one of the five groups showed profits. Three outperformed the Dow Jones Industrial Average decisively. The *average* of all these group gains, after counting in the sluggish performance of oil stocks and the minus figures for steel and iron equities, was a tremendous 51.9 percent, compared to 5.9 percent for the Dow Jones yardstick of the whole market.

BUY MANAGEMENT

One of my friends is a history buff and football fan. He has a theory that there are no good generals, only lucky ones. Ditto football coaches. I have not heard his ideas on the role of corporate management in making a company click or fizzle and don't agree with him in any case. Where the Duke of Wellington, Julius Caesar, Marlborough, and other military brains went, battles were won against big odds. And while Bear Bryant coached the University of Kentucky, Kentucky won. When he moved to Texas A & M, the Aggie teams swept their conference. Alabama, the Bear's present domicile, is a place of powerhouse football. In the pro ranks, coaches like Paul Brown and Don Shula produce winners wherever they travel.

So with investing. The good managers win. Their companies produce profits, their operations are lean, their sales forces hungry. Their stockholders are often happy people.

In the case of buying management, all you can do is attempt to measure progress of a corporation under a management group. This is imprecise. But so is measurement of the coaching abilities of Bear Bryant and Paul Brown. Yet such study pays off.

SEEK TRENDS

Humans are habit-bound. When they finally do change, the new ways become mores which in turn are slow to be replaced. It's that way with the trends of tastes, wants, and ways which influence corporate profits and in turn make or break the prices of corporate stocks.

Today the automobile is criticized for polluting the air, clogging the highways, making city streets impassable. Twenty years ago, to have a bigger, better, more accessory-laden vehicle than one's neighbor was to have achieved the pinnacle of neighborhood leadership. It took many years to put cars on top of the symbol heap and more years for them to roll off into the slough of disrepute.

If you can spot new trends of this kind there is plenty of time to climb aboard and plenty of profit when you turn out to be right. Unlike the effort to judge management skill, in researching trends you have some solid information as guideposts.

The University of Michigan at Ann Arbor publishes data on its highly regarded surveys of consumer buying intentions and will sell you a subscription. You can also ask for *Consumer Buying Prospects,* a quarterly free report of Commercial Credit Co., 300 St. Paul Place, Baltimore, Md. This indicates actual and projected consumer spending for new automobiles, major household durables, and single family dwellings, with breakdowns by purchase item and region.

Just as important as consumer plans are social trends and the trends of government spending. Aircraft-aerospace companies were big investments in the days when major government emphasis was on their products. Then the trends changed; government became more interested in social than military projects. The aerospace companies, fallen upon evil times, became traps for unwary investors who had not understood changed times and new emphasis. It is that way with all governmental spending trends. Spot those, observe the directions of court decisions, watch what politicians say and the things for which they vote appropriations, and you will be able to see new profit avenues opening. It is not likely that the role of government in setting economic and other directions will alter in the decade ahead. It may become total.

Observe social as well as political trends. In an age when the young turn away from frills and geegaws to simpler ways, the outlook for industries making many peripheral products is not such as to make them attractive trend-riders.

Social aims of the whole body politic should be studied. If there is determination to unblight the cities and to provide better living for disadvantaged citizens, then companies in industries which provide such merchandise and services ought to be important profit-makers.

The above should not be taken to mean that young people will always turn against the status symbols of an establishment they reject, or even that they will always reject it. Nor should it be taken to mean that the social directions will remain identical with those at the moment this is written. What matters is not the two above examples, but that investors should seek *trends*.

SHARP TIMING

Charts don't foretell the future. They picture the past. Yet in those pictures skilled chart readers can detect turning points while they are still small and offer maximum opportunity for buying (when the chart indicates the start of an upswing) or selling (when it shows a rising trend beginning to flounder over into a decline).

The people who were least hurt in the bad market times of 1969 and 1970 and the confused market of 1971 were the chart readers. "If nothing else, the charts told us when to get out and do nothing," said one analyst. "Sometimes the most profitable ploy is to stay on the sidelines."

For most practical purposes, the explanation which follows will equip you with sufficient skill to read the chart books in your broker's office knowledgeably:

If you draw on a piece of chart paper a vertical line which represents the range of the period under study (day, week, or month), with a cross mark on that vertical line denoting the closing price, you will have the beginnings of the common bar chart.

The chart will indicate that within the market there are buying forces that have in the past brought enough buying power into the market to repeatedly stop a decline at a certain point. Other signs indicate that there are selling forces eager to unload stocks at another price.

In general, the bar chartist observes the upward zigs and downward zags which form a trend. From those, and with the help of a number of rules worked out by experience, he attempts to spot a trend.

Support and resistance study underlies all technical study. If a stock, moving upward, stops at 45, churns a day or so, and then declines over a period of two or three weeks to the level of 40, a technician would predict that the stock will meet "resistance" at 45 on the next up-move. The technician knows that two things happened previously at the price level of 45: The demand from bulls dried up and the resistance of bears, evidenced by selling activity, increased. It is logical, he believes, to expect that some of the bears who wanted to unload at 45 will not have succeeded the last time; these bears will be waiting, stock certificates in hand, at the barricade of 45 for another opportunity to unload at what they consider an advantageous price.

If prices do push above the level of resistance, a technician knows that the bears have been overwhelmed by bulls as bulls' dollars clear the way for a further advance, at least for a time. If prices in this hypothetical situation move up to the 45 level, fail to penetrate it and retreat, and a further assault mounted by buyers at last hurdles the 45 level with increased volume, the chartist would become excited. From his lines on ruled paper, he would deduce that a large block of overhanding stock had been bought by bulls, thus increasing the likelihood of a sizable advance.

A "support" level is a resistance level in reverse. If, in a bottom area, sufficient buying to stem a decline is introduced into the market, a technician would use the same type of reasoning as he did on the appearance of resistance to an up-move, but in reverse.

Whereas the bar chart contains time, volume, and price, the point-and-figure chart works with price only. And even there it works with price *changes* only.

The point-and-figure man reasons this way: Price trends are generated out of congested periods during which prices reverse themselves back and forth, eating up the monetary ammunition of stock buyers and the equity ammunition of stock sellers. Therefore, what matters is to chart these reversals.

Thus, the point-and-figure analyst enters successive price figures in an upward column as long as prices continue to go up. When there is a change of significant size, the figures move to another column and are entered in downward progressions until there is a significant upward change. Thus the X's march across the chart paper.

Although he has a different set of names for the patterns which appear on his charts, the point-and-figure analyst also works with support and resistance areas and with a tool not afforded by a bar chart: the "count." By counting the squares across a congestion area (the point-and-figure term for what bar chartists term a trading range), the point-and-figure analyst claims that he can tell with reasonable—although not exact—accuracy how far the move which follows a breakout is likely to occur. The really expert point-and-figure people have some very good records in this respect. (For more information on charting, see my *How To Chart Your Way to Stock Market Profits,* 1967, Parker Publishing Co., to be reprinted in paperback by Arco Publishing Co.).

Another group of technical analysts works with momentum, sometimes called relative-strength study. The object is to spot securities which are moving with more momentum than the market as a whole. The rationale behind momentum study is that the object in swift motion is likely to continue to move rapidly. Momentum study is applied by many analysts particularly to the study of industry groups in order to spot the "in" industries which enjoy greatest investor favor. Coupled with other technical disciplines, momentum study has much to offer.

A number of statistical services publish computerized momentum studies, giving the stocks which have performed worst and best over varying lengths of time. Watch the position of a stock on each of three lists. If a stock is the tenth-best performer on the list of seven-week momentum, third-best on the three-week list, and second or even first on the one-week momentum list, its velocity is increasing. It might be a good buy, at least for a quick turn. Computer services' ads are found in financial media, including *Barron's,* the *Wall Street Journal, The New York Times,* and *Forbes.*

Nothing in the above exposition of technical methods implies infallibility. You can lose on stocks chosen by technical methods. Yet they are generally useful, often the most meaningful of many studies, and always a useful added tool to apply with other methods of choosing stocks.

THE UNPOPULARITY TECHNIQUE

Some analysts have developed special techniques which fly in the face of established Wall Street wisdom by calling for an investor to purchase a stock at the nadir of unpopularity.

One researcher studied results of buying stocks with lowest price-earnings ratios (PER) among the thirty Dow Jones Industrial Average components. A low PER is a sign of small regard; investors, some of whom at least are supposedly well informed and all of whom influence stock prices in some degree by their purchases and sales, are willing to capitalize the earnings of such a company at lesser multiples than they apply to corporation stocks from which they expect better things. The PER is computed by dividing earnings into price. If a stock earns $1 per share and sells at 8, its ratio is 8. High ratios generally indicate greater regard.

This researcher's computer "invested" money in the ten stocks having lowest PER's. Then he reinvested proceeds once a year in stocks that at the new date had the smallest multiples. He did this through a theoretical 25-year period. The starting "capital" was $10,000. Over a quarter-century this appreciated to $119,198, outstripping other theoretical portfolio techniques.

In another study, stocks were bought after they had just cut dividend payouts, a time of maximum unpopularity. Stocks in this computer study decisively outperformed the wide market averages.

A third researcher put his computer to work sorting out stocks of companies which were running deficits instead of profits. Over a period, 1948–1967, these, if bought when deficits were reported, would during two or three subsequent years have performed on average better than other stocks.

BLUE CHIPS—NOT BLUE SKY

In poker, the highest monetary value is generally assigned to blue chips. From this custom, the stocks of staid, heart-of-the-economy companies that were big, at least partly proof against damage in declines that might sink smaller outfits, and financially strong enough to operate in a big league where money is counted in nine figures, came to be called blue chips. In the seventies, they are a better place to put your money than in the blue-sky stocks, those with nothing but hopes and boasts which reach up to the sky. There are three reasons for this.

The first is that blue-chip companies are made of solid substance. In a time of lessening prosperity the companies with real operating units, sales forces capable of putting their goods into stores and consumers' shelves, and factories that are producing and not still ironing out production bugs can survive. The company which lacks such substance has small hope. It may be farming out production; in such case its added cost layer must tell when the competitive struggle gets hot. It may be producing more dreams than products in a factory not yet shaken down to low-cost operation. It may be in an area suddenly experiencing labor or other troubles; competing under that condition with a blue-chip firm having plants in many areas will prove disastrous. The size of blue-chip companies is a reason why they will prove sounder investments.

A second reason for blue-chip preference is their financial muscle. A small company has trouble in the best of times going against the big outfit's research and development. If a project fails to work out, the blue chip is little the worse for that fact. The blue-sky firm can be financially wrecked. Research and development (R & D) in a blue-chip company are necessarily wider because there is more money to support wide-ranging research, out of which more and better products are likely to come.

A third argument is the visibility of blue-chip companies. It was possible for many blue-sky-growth companies to commit repeated hanky-panky with their earnings and other statistics, partly because they were less visible. They had fewer stockholders, few analysts to pick accounting entries apart (although during the growth frenzy, there were hardly any analysts *able* to pick apart phony accounting), and less look-over-the-shoulder from market regulators. The blue-chip companies must operate in full sunlight. Their bookkeeping entries are not invariably honest or the executives' public statements always candid and complete, but there is greater likelihood of honesty and less possibility for hanky-panky.

These reasons for blue-chip preference apply under all kinds of conditions. Even in the free-swinging days of the 1960's, few glamorous electronic firms could show the R & D results of an American Telephone and Telegraph. Computer companies came and went while the giant blue-chip International Business Machines continued to prosper. The chemical industry's *wunderkinder* of an early time went under, while in the tough-industry days of the later sixties, duPont, Monsanto, and Allied Chemical plowed ahead.

Consider figures which compare the 1969–1970 bear-market lows in blue-sky stocks with their highs during the preceding bull market, and a similar comparison for blue-chip equities in the same industries:

While it was a favorite, the blue-sky stock of Denny's Restaurants had a top of 53. The stock dropped to 8 at its bear-market low for a loss of 85 percent. Kentucky Fried Chicken had a lofty 56 top, from which it slid to a 17 low in May, 1970. Investors lost 69 percent.

On the other hand, blue-chip General Foods was 47 during the bull-market frenzy of 1967–1968, and 33 at the May, 1970, low. The 30 percent loss hurt, but not nearly as badly as the catastrophic declines in Kentucky Fried and Denny's. Moreover, General Foods quickly bounced back close to its earlier high.

If the medical field interested an investor during the bull phase preceding the 1969–1970 drop, he could have held such speculative, hopeful stocks as Medic-Home Enterprises or United Convalescent Hospitals. The action was in nursing homes at that time. These sold at bull highs of 40 and 32, respectively. Medic-Home dropped to a low of 4 in May, 1970, for a 90 percent loss. United Convalescent Hospitals declined to 2 for a 94 percent loss.

However, an investor interested in the growth of health care *might* have opted during the bull market of 1967–1968 for blue chips on the order of Smith, Kline and French Laboratories or Pfizer, Inc. While high-flying Medic-Home and United Convalescent were selling at their 40 and 32 levels, Smith, Kline and French saw a high of 65 and Pfizer 30. Their May, 1970, lows were at 37 and 26 for losses of 7.5 percent and 13 percent. From these lows, both blue-chip medical stocks went on to new highs in 1970.

In electronic data processing University Computing was a high flyer at a lofty price of 187. From that level it sank to 21 in May, 1970, for an 88 percent loss. During the same period, blue-chip International Business Machines showed a high-to-low decline of 42 percent.

In October, 1971, two professors from midwestern universities released a study on the relative performance of blue-chip and blue-sky stocks over an extended period. It was titled *Risk, Return, Diversification, and the Resurrection of Purchasing Power Risk*. Robert A. Haugen, assistant professor of finance at the University of Wisconsin Graduate School of Business, and A. James Heins, University of Illinois economist, charted price movements and dividend payouts of 150 New York Stock Exchange securities over a 44-year test period. They reported that, over the long haul, blue chips outperformed the "performance" type of speculative securities.

Their study compared dividend returns plus capital gain to the initial purchase price. Only 60 of the 150 issues were still in existence at the end of the 44-year study period. Some died, some were merged into other companies. Each was replaced on its disappearance with another security.

Of the survivors, the best rates of return were made by International Business Machines, General Electric, Eastman Kodak, Sears, Roebuck, and Brown Shoe. All possessed "growth," but none could be equated with the rapid-increase, quick-decline type of "growth" equity so much favored during the madness of the sixties. Except for IBM, all had been relegated to the blue-chip back shelf during that mania for fast augmentation in per share earnings and for stocks that could double in six months and quadruple in a year.

The stock market runs in phases almost as regular as the in-out, ebb-and-flow movements of ocean tides. One of its trends is the movement from bull to bear. During a strongly up movement, most stocks are carried to higher levels. During a bear trend when the notion of investment in stocks is out of favor, even good securities go down. The market has another in-out type of pulsation tied to phases of favor for blue chips and for blue-sky stocks.

When a bull movement begins in the despair and wreckage of a bear-market bottom, investors, burned and careful, often stay within the safer shelter of blue-chip stocks. As the bull movement gathers strength and stretches itself out in time, these investors lose a little of their fear. Memory of past losses grows dim. New investors, unfamiliar with stocks and unburned by earlier bear-market losses, are attracted to the market. The investing taste laps over to take in some speculative blue-sky issues. As profits build and memories of bear troubles recede, the blue chips begin to be dumped so that investors can put more of their money into blue-sky issues, which at the moment are performing well. Finally, all the action is in blue-sky stocks.

Then the bull market turns over and stocks fall. Still the blue chips don't come into favor. Investors believe the market's recent events. Later, repeatedly hurt by this trust in growth stocks, they at last lose interest in all stocks. With the burnout of the innocents, a bear-market bottoms and, not immediately but eventually, a new bull market starts a slow rise from the levels of disappointment and bankruptcy.

The year 1932 saw the worst beating any American market ever took. From that bottom, nearly thirty years were required for an interest in blue-sky stocks to take hold once more. A generation of investors had to come along, unacquainted with bear troubles and unscarred by the traumatic 1929–1932 mess.

The madness for growth seen in the sixties was a rebirth of this interest in blue sky. Blue-sky stocks are likely to lead only to trouble for the foreseeable future; safety and potential investment profits lie elsewhere.

"GROWTH" AND BLUE-CHIP STATUS TOO?

Take a good look at food stocks, banks, and utilities. Each of these operates in an area where more than one governmental regulatory body stands around waiting for its accountants to make a slip on which some eager young staff lawyer can pounce. Some of them are in fields where dozens of commissions, committees, and boards look over their shoulders. And each is close to the heart of the economy. Things have to become pretty bleak before consumers stop using banks' facilities or begin to read by candlelight or eat less.

Examine the record of these stock groups for producing price appreciation despite their stodgy image:

In one special report on bank stocks, the securities firm of Keefe, Bruyette and Woods, Inc. noted that for the decade March, 1960, to March, 1970, the Dow Jones Industrial Average, which most people equate with the market, appreciated 28 percent. A Keefe, Bruyette and Woods average of bank stocks appreciated 90 percent in the same period. The Dow Jones Utility Average, companion yardstick to the Industrials, went up 33 percent. During this period *Barron's* average of food stocks appreciated 46 percent.

Bank stocks and utilities also outperformed the Industrial Average in annual compounded growth rate of dividends. Dividend growth for the Industrial Average was 4.5 percent a year on average. It was 6.9 percent for the Keefe banks and 5.4 percent for utilities.

The following view about utilities was presented by industry specialist William Haugen of Merrill Lynch, Pierce, Fenner and Smith at an informal discussion with that firm's registered representatives held in early 1971:

> Demand for electrical energy will continue to increase in the future, and its growth rate might well accelerate. The outlook for an expansion of housing continues to be bright; although types of construction may vary, climate conditioning is moving toward much wider acceptance. Commercial use also should rise as a broader affluence pervades the marketplace. In addition to the additional power used by industry to meet competition, a promising new market still in its infancy is the use of electric energy in various devices and processes concerned with pollution control and ecology. Many of those problems can be alleviated or eliminated by means of the use of pumps and other motors as the effluent or gas is moved toward clarification or purification.

It is not necessary to present a case for continued growth of food consumption in a nation with continuing population growth, other than to point out that in the food field, as in electronics or data processing, steady, dependable growth is likely to be found in blue chips rather than blue-sky stocks during a period when competition is expected to be tight and risks for marginal businesses high.

ROTATE BLUE CHIPS

For ten years, dividends of Scott Paper Company, mightiest maker of toilet tissues, rose steadily if unspectacularly from 75 cents per share to $1.00. Scott had once been hailed as the very model of a modern growth company. Then in 1971 an event happened which would have been unbelievable a decade earlier. Scott cut the dividend in half, from 25 cents per share to 12½ cents, citing "extraordinary capital demands."

By no coincidence, the financial newspaper which reported this event also carried a feature article telling how in its stronghold field of toilet tissues, Scott had been flushed from leadership by bigger, mightier Procter and Gamble, new to the paper industry but an old hand at stocking supermarket shelves. Moving fast into the toweling and tissue field, P & G had taken over Scott's former dominating role.

Both were blue chips. One prospered at the other's expense, pointing up the necessity for investors to rotate even blue-chip investments rather than allow them to stagnate. The fact of a company's heart-of-economy position must not delude investors intent on success in the coming years into belief that old ways which worked will always do so.

The thirty components of the Dow Jones Industrial are large companies. Most analysts concede them blue-chip status. Rotation of interest and profit-potential in this diversified group of blue-chip stocks was wide during the booming times of 1956–1965. Table 1 of relative position, showing which stock performed first in the group, which second, which fifth, which thirtieth, is revealing.

TABLE 1. PERFORMANCE RANK OF THIRTY DOW JONES COMPONENTS

Company	1956	1957	1958	1959	1960	1961	1962	1963	1964	1965
International Nickel	1	28	22	9	7	3	26	23	11	16
Goodyear	2	8	12	17	21	10	25	5	20	17
U.S. Steel	3	26	1	24	22	21	30	8	27	19
United Aircraft	4	25	29	30	14	18	2	30	1	1
Bethlehem Steel	5	24	11	23	25	20	28	24	16	11
Std. Oil (N.J.)	6	15	27	27	18	14	4	3	13	27
Johns-Manville	7	20	13	26	5	27	23	18	19	18
Eastman Kodak	8	2	10	2	8	26	10	22	8	2
Std. Oil (Calif.)	9	12	19	29	12	16	3	29	6	14
Intl. Harvester	10	27	3	14	17	15	11	9	7	8
General Electric	11	7	21	7	23	25	7	17	21	6
Aluminum Co. of America	12	29	4	18	26	29	15	6	30	7
Union Carbide	13	17	17	16	20	24	17	11	22	15
Anaconda	14	30	5	22	29	19	16	15	18	4
Procter & Gamble	15	3	18	12	1	7	21	20	23	30
Texaco	16	6	14	25	10	6	6	19	5	26
Westinghouse Elec.	17	4	28	1	15	30	18	26	9	3
General Motors	18	21	7	20	24	4	8	2	10	13
American Tel. & Tel.	19	10	16	21	3	12	14	12	16	28
Owens-Illinois	20	11	9	13	16	22	22	13	12	9
General Foods	21	1	6	3	2	5	19	16	29	20
International Paper	22	18	15	15	28	17	24	1	24	25
Woolworth	23	16	8	8	9	8	27	14	17	12
American Tobacco	24	5	23	19	4	2	29	27	14	22
American Can	25	9	25	28	19	9	9	28	25	5
Allied Chemical	26	23	20	11	13	23	20	7	28	23
DuPont	27	13	26	10	27	11	5	21	15	10
Chrysler	28	22	30	4	30	13	1	1	2	29
Swift & Co.	29	19	24	5	11	28	12	25	3	25
Sears, Roebuck	30	14	2	6	6	1	13	4	4	21

Table 2 indicates dollar results of the rotation of interest among blue-chip components of the venerable Dow Jones Average. It is taken from the 1970 edition of *Investor's Guide* put out by Investment Company of America.

The advantages of rotating investments from a poor performer to a top performer become obvious—even (perhaps especially) when dealing with blue-chip stocks of high quality and wide marketability.

At the end of every year look over the blue-chip stocks you possess and grade each for long-term performance, starting with the time you bought it, and for intermediate results based upon the time elapsed since the last grading.

Ask yourself regarding each poor performer: "Did this stock do badly because of past conditions which no longer apply? Or

TABLE 2. INVESTING IN COMMON STOCKS REQUIRES SKILL

The difficulty of selecting individual stocks is illustrated by the wide variation in the results shown below of assumed investments 36 years ago in each of the 30 stocks now in the Dow Jones Industrial Average.

Company	Market value of investment* January 1, 1934	December 31, 1969	Percent of gain
Eastman Kodak	$10,000	$659,617	6,496
International Paper	10,000	452,029	4,420
Sears, Roebuck	10,000	391,718	3,817
Goodyear Tire & Rubber	10,000	251,425	2,414
Texaco	10,000	229,596	2,196
Procter & Gamble	10,000	170,708	1,607
Westinghouse Electric	10,000	130,518	1,205
General Electric	10,000	119,231	1,092
General Motors	10,000	116,831	1,068
Aluminum Company of America	10,000	115,891	1,059
General Foods	10,000	102,308	923
Standard Oil (New Jersey)	10,000	99,238	892
International Nickel	10,000	98,864	889
Bethlehem Steel	10,000	87,973	780
duPont	10,000	84,035	740
United Aircraft	10,000	83,571	736
Standard Oil of California	10,000	77,377	674
Owens-Illinois	10,000	61,235	512
Johns-Manville	10,000	59,504	495
Chrysler	10,000	49,631	396
Union Carbide	10,000	46,737	367
Swift	10,000	43,103	331
U.S. Steel	10,000	42,408	324
Anaconda	10,000	41,197	312
International Harvester	10,000	37,125	271
Woolworth (F.W.)	10,000	26,185	162
American Telephone	10,000	26,137	161
American Brands	10,000	20,613	106
American Can	10,000	16,515	65
Allied Chemical	10,000	15,096	51

* It was assumed that the full $10,000 was invested in each stock and that fractional shares were purchased where required to use up the full amount. No brokerage charges were included in cost. Adjustments were made for all stock splits and stock dividends.

because of current conditions which are likely to stretch out into the period ahead?"

If your answer leans toward "yes" on the second question, it is time to rotate the stock and look for a better blue-chip performer.

Chapter 4

THE REAL PLACE
OF MUTUAL FUNDS

Each investor will cite a different advantage of mutual funds. Each is right in a narrow, restricted way, but lacks an overall view of the fund industry and its part in intelligent investing for our changed times.

INVESTORS' DEFINITIONS OF MUTUAL FUNDS

"Mutual funds are like a security blanket. They give you the feeling of hiding away from all the dangers that stocks and bonds offer."

"Mutual funds are a way to build toward happy retirement in later years." (A few insist that funds are a way to make sure retirement will be meager and pinched; these are the investors who hoped for much from the go-go funds which manufactured false asset values in the sixties.)

"Mutual funds are like a pro football team. Their professional managers know what to do just as the coach of the Baltimore Colts knows his business." (Coaches, like mutual fund managers, sometimes goof.)

"The mutual fund is like home insulation which keeps the cold out. A fund makes investors safe from the blowing winds and drenching rains of a bad bear season."

"Mutual funds are like a bank. They maintain your savings safely."

"Mutual funds are a hedge to beat inflation. American industry has to prosper—if you don't believe that, where are you?—and as it does, the mutual funds that own a slice of this big land's factories have to prosper too. Inflation might go on, but you'll be ahead if you bet on America through its mutual funds." (A red, white, and blue view.)

"Without mutual funds a small investor could not achieve diversification." (Ask a stockholder of Mates Fund about that theory; he didn't lose all his eggs when Mates' basket came unwoven, but he lost most of them.)

"Mutual funds give the little investor a chance to get rich." (Enterprise Fund at the end of 1968 had enjoyed many straight years of sizable net-asset-value increases and had once led the pack as the mutual fund that gained most of all over a twelve-month stretch. Then came the demise of letter stocks and a dearth of interest in hotshot little companies with small capitalizations such as cluttered Enterprise's portfolio. Enterprise stockholders, whose shares were valued at $9.68 in mid-1968, watched them dwindle to $8.98 in mid-1969 and to $5.00 at the midpoint of 1970. But July 1, 1971, with most of the market well up from the 1970 lows and reaching for a top, Enterprise shares were only $6.73, losing $3.05 or 31 percent in three years of getting rich.)

Mutuals do have these values, but each in itself misses the mark. Mutuals are, indeed, a method of achieving security. They furnish diversification among many stocks and a number of industries such as no ordinary investor of moderate means could achieve. They furnish professional management, often better (but sometimes much worse) than amateurish efforts an investor might achieve alone. To an extent—although not a big one—they can insulate against risks of a declining market. Some people have become rich through mutual fund investing, and some have grown poor.

The glamor has worn off the once shiny mutual fund idea. Investors have realized that mutuals don't always furnish wise management, nor always well-planned diversification, nor do they give anybody a security blanket in this insecure world. When people saw that funds were fallible, a disillusionment began which produced, among other effects, a wave of selling that hit funds in 1971.

A study by the Twentieth Century Fund concluded that during the 1960's mutual fund activity produced much of the up-down swinging activity the market saw in those years. Arthur F. Burns, Chairman of the Board of Governors of the Federal Reserve System, has noted:

"A major source of the speculative ardor came from some parts of the mutual fund industry. Long-term investment in stocks of companies with proven earnings records became an outmoded concept for the new breed of 'go-go' funds. The 'smart money' was to go into issues of technologically oriented firms—no matter how they were meeting the test of profitability, or into the corporate conglomerates—no matter how eccentric their character."

Yet the funds do have an important place in intelligent investing for the difficult years ahead. We're going to examine that place shortly. First, however, a look at mutuals with the blinders off.

(1) Mutuals are still mighty. They dispose of a vast amount of capital entrusted to them by small, and a few large, investors. Their holdings are not as sizable as those of some other institutions. Pension funds have more money. So do the insurance companies. Nobody knows exactly how much stock-purchasing power is in the hands of bank trust departments. But none of these institutions exerts as much effect upon stock prices as do mutuals. The reason is that pension funds, trust department portfolios, and insurance companies do not put all their money into common stocks. These bigger, older institutions also buy land, buildings, mortgages, bonds. With only minor exceptions, the mutual funds invest primarily in common stocks.

(2) Mutuals are not always run by staid, conservative people, although this may have once been true. The mutual fund industry still offers some of the wildest, swingingest speculations this side of Las Vegas. These have a place in tomorrow's investing. But you have to know what you're doing.

(3) Mutual funds will come back into favor. It was the misdeeds of a minority which brought about current investor dis-

trust. The mutual fund idea is too good to die out; anything which meets a real human need must survive. The funds do meet such a need.

LESSONS TAUGHT BY PAST FAILURES OF FUNDS

First decide where you're going before you choose a vehicle for getting there. Some investors wish to achieve big gains, taking big risks in order to do so. This is a sound procedure for certain people. But others need to invest conservatively in order to keep their capital from shriveling. Still others require high current income to supplement their retirement checks, social security, or salary. Before determining upon a fund, an investor must find out whether it is going toward the destination at which he wants to arrive. No point in buying an income fund for speculation or a fund investing in new ventures when steady, dependable quarterly dividends are required. Some of the failures resulted from investors neglecting to find a right fund for their purposes.

Read the fine print. Legally, no fund shares may be sold an investor unless he receives the dull, lengthy piece of literature called a prospectus. Most people put it aside and concentrate upon the charts which show how a theoretical investor of a decade ago might have fared if he had put $10,000 into Wingbat Limited Fund (theoretical mutual fund investors always put $10,000, no more or less, into fund purchases ten years ago). The prospectus is dull. It exists for investors' protection, however. If an investor lured by Mates Fund in its palmy days had seen the words "restricted securities" *and taken the trouble to inquire what that phrase meant,* he might have been spared a monetary bloodbath in addition to worry during the long period when there were no redemptions of Mates shares.

Today, restricted securities are clearly labeled and a considerable number of safeguards have grown up to protect investors from a recurrence of asset fattening by means of unsalable securities bought at discounts. But there will be other gimmicks and new ways of making things appear to be what they are not. No legal safeguards have ever protected investors from clever people able to weave a new idea into the tissue of existing regulations.

I don't know what the next gimmick may be. I do know that if you read the prospectus carefully before buying a mutual fund, and question any matter not fully explained, you will be warned away from danger—whatever it is. Examine footnotes especially. These usually spell out the dangers hidden by the figures printed in larger type.

Not all mutual funds employ gimmicks. But some do, and always will. The prospectus protects you.

When you want to gamble, go to Nevada. The deflation of funds devoted to speculation has not stopped investors from purchasing new ones. There are funds for letter stocks; funds that buy up art treasures (selling to whom?); funds for speculation in commodities such as wheat, copper, soybeans, or orange juice; funds for nearly any speculative project. If you buy such funds you should understand that you are engaging in outright gambling, not investment. Funds which gambled fared poorly even in the markets of the 1960's. They are likely to fare worse in the tougher times ahead.

Wall Street's mutuals have a percentage and it does not work in your favor. Whether devoted to buying stocks, Cézannes, or soybeans, this mutual fund percentage comes in the form of a loading-charge commission accompanied by management fees and the commissions paid art dealers, commodity exchanges, and so forth for buying and selling. That fixed, continuing cost will wreck any gambling program in far-out objects which you hope to see go up in scarcity value. Moreover, the managements which charge you fees aren't always professional. Often their knowledge and performance records are so poor that if they ran racehorses instead of objets d'art, it would be necessary to hang out lanterns at night for the nags to find their way home.

Mutual funds should be used for investment, not gambling.

New ways are not always better. The old way to run a fund was to invest in bonds and blue-chip stocks with the idea that a prudent man, or a widow or orphan would be furnished maximum protection with, it was hoped, some worthwhile amount of current income and, in days of rising markets, some appreciation of capital. Then came the tulipomania of the sixties. Suddenly it was thought too stodgy to seek everyday objectives. The new idea was to swing. The small investors swung—and fell.

In years ahead other "new" ways of doing things will hit the mutual fund field. Some will be good and should be followed. Many will be busts and should be avoided. Each idea should be appraised for its worth rather than for its newness and its promise of producing fast gains.

Move entirely out of mutuals at certain times. In chapter 12 we will examine ways that thoughtful Wall Street analysts have developed for determining when a little, wiggling decline in stock prices might be the first wave of a horrifying backward tide. At such times, mutual funds should be dumped along with stocks. An investor able to spot downward trends finds that his capital, conserved from the catastrophe, buys more shares so that the swings of bull and bear trends not only fail to cause loss but serve as a means for capital enhancement.

Conservatively managed Massachusetts Investors Trust is the big daddy of open-end load funds (an explanation of open-end funds appears later in this chapter). MIT shareowners possessed $16.55 in net-asset value per share in mid-1967. This shrank to $11.68 by mid-1970 despite MIT's vaunted team of analysts and managers presumably able to spot big bear traps such as that in 1969–1970. By mid-1971, with the market nearly back to the earlier top areas, MIT shares had recovered only to a net-asset value of $14.32.

The investor who had wisely sold 100 MIT shares around the mid-1968 top of $17.15, realizing $1,715, would have been able to re-buy 135 shares at $12.70 ($11.68 plus standard front-end loading charge commission). When these appreciated back to $14.32 one year later, the investor would have increased his capital of $1,715, which he cashed in 1968, to $2,219.60.

It paid then—and will again—to sell out on bearish indications rather than wait for fund management to protect you. The fund managers can't do it even if they are able to spot bear trends (not all possess or employ the important market timing tools we're going to discuss in a coming chapter). They cannot sell out because their holdings are too large. Mutual funds in 1968 possessed about $55 billion in assets. No existing market machinery would have absorbed such widespread selling without breakdown and financial chaos.

Watch (and watch out for) loading charges. The front-end loading charge is a commission based upon percentage of the net-asset value of a mutual fund. It is added to net-asset value so that when you buy shares of a load fund you're likely to be purchasing a good deal less in true value than you pay for. Not all mutual funds charge a front-end commission. Those that do are called load funds. Those that do not are called no-loads.

The argument for the loading charge is that this reimburses a dealer and his salesman for the "service" they render to an investor by going out to sell him mutual fund shares. Both load and no-load funds assess management fees for running the fund and both pay brokerage commissions when they buy and sell stocks for the fund's portfolio. The difference in "service," therefore, is in having salesmen push load funds while you have to buy no-loads on your own without benefit of high-pressure tactics and in-home calls.

In and after the 1969–1970 debacle, premier performance was sometimes turned in by the no-loads, which were cheaper to buy although less well known because they were sold without salesmen. You'll have to read ads in financial journals to get the addresses of no-loads.

CLOSED-END AND OPEN-END FUNDS

Another basic variation among mutual funds is the distinction between closed-end and open-end funds.

A closed-end fund has a set number of shares, unless the number is increased or decreased with the approval of the shareholders, after which the new number becomes set. Such a fund is initially sold to the public in the way that a fresh issue of corporate stock would be sold. The shares are then traded in the manner of corporation stock. If you buy or sell stock in a closed-end fund you pay the same standard stock commissions that you'd pay to buy or sell General Motors.

A closed-end fund trades stocks in and out of its portfolio, paying commissions to do so. These commissions become a cost of operation borne by the shareholders of the fund. Management charges a fixed fee for running the fund.

Open-end funds have floating capitalizations. Each day they stand ready to buy shares from investors who want to cash up, and to sell new shares to those who want to join the family of stockholders. They generally cash up at net-asset value per share. Sometimes a charge is assessed. No-load funds will sell new shares at asset value. Load funds charge a front-end commission as dues for admitting members to their club.

While open-end funds sell at asset value with or without the addition of a front-end loading charge, shares of closed-end funds trade at a price frequently unconnected with the underlying value of the shares. These shares frequently sell at a discount from asset value. This tends to create the appearance of a bargain. The appearance can be misleading because many closed-ends continue trading at discounts year after year, so that the shares bought as a bargain because of the discount end up being sold at another discount. On occasion, however, closed-end shares trade up to asset value and even, at rare times, at a premium above asset value. This occurs when investors believe the future of the fund or of the area in which it invests is so great as to justify a premium. It is nearly always unwise to buy closed-ends at premium, but sometimes wise to buy at discounts from asset value.

Table 3 shows the variance of prices of closed-end funds above and below asset values on a typical day, October 22, 1971.

There is one unusual breed of closed-end. Under certain circumstances tremendous leverage (a subject to be covered in detail in Chapter 7) is afforded in dual funds. The capitalization of dual funds consists of "income" and "capital" shares. All dividends and interest paid by portfolio securities are given (after management fees) to the income shareowner. If the portfolio increases in value, all gains are credited to the capital shareowner who must bear the loss of any depreciation in capital values of the dual fund's portfolio. The income shares of dual funds tend to be fairly stable, valued more on going yield rates than on fluctuation in underlying net-asset value. The capital shares can gyrate wildly and, like other closed-ends, sometimes trade at wide discounts from, or premiums above, asset values. On the date that Table 3, showing variations in orthodox closed-end funds, was compiled, Table 4 was prepared for a group of dual-purpose funds.

Whether open-end or closed-end, a fund has an aim and a way it accomplishes that aim. To use funds intelligently in the era

TABLE 3. VARIATIONS IN VALUES AND PRICES OF CLOSED-END FUNDS

Fund	Net-asset value	Stock price	Percent difference
Adams Express	14.54	$12\frac{3}{8}$	−14.9
American European	41.73	39	− 6.5
American General Bond	24.69	$26\frac{5}{8}$	+ 7.8
American–South African	27.81	$38\frac{7}{8}$	+39.8
Amoskeag	67.52	48	−28.9
Bancroft	22.95	$21\frac{1}{2}$	− 6.3
Carriers	18.72	$15\frac{1}{4}$	−18.5
Diebold	9.81	$5\frac{1}{2}$	−43.9
Dominick	11.09	$8\frac{1}{4}$	−25.6
General American Investors	24.34	23	− 5.5
International Holdings	17.83	$13\frac{7}{8}$	−22.2
Japan Fund	8.32	$9\frac{1}{2}$	+14.2
J. Hancock	23.65	$22\frac{3}{4}$	− 3.8
Lehman	17.43	$16\frac{1}{2}$	− 5.3
Madison	14.98	$14\frac{1}{2}$	− 3.2
National Aviation	26.30	$21\frac{7}{8}$	−16.8
Niagara Shares	15.72	$15\frac{3}{4}$	+ 0.2
Overseas Securities	5.87	$7\frac{7}{8}$	+34.1
Petroleum Corp.	20.97	$18\frac{5}{8}$	−11.2
Standard Shares	28.54	$23\frac{1}{4}$	−18.5
Surveyor Fund	6.76	$5\frac{1}{8}$	−24.1
Tri-Continental	33.08	$27\frac{5}{8}$	−16.5
United	11.40	8	−29.8
U.S. & Foreign Securities	34.68	$32\frac{3}{8}$	− 6.6

TABLE 4. VARIATIONS IN PRICES AND VALUES OF CAPITAL SHARES OF DUAL-PURPOSE FUNDS

Dual-Purpose Fund	Capital shares		Percent difference
	Price	Net-asset value	
Am. DualVest	$8\frac{1}{2}$	9.55	−11.0
Gemini	$14\frac{1}{4}$	18.3	−19.0
Hemisphere	4	3.51	−19.0
Income and capital	$10\frac{1}{4}$	13.87	−26.1
Leverage	$10\frac{3}{4}$	15.34	−29.9
Putnam Duo Fund	5	6.38	−21.6
Scudder Duo-Vest	$6\frac{1}{4}$	8.52	−26.6
Scudder D-V Exchange	35	41.38	−15.4

ahead, you will have to judge the following in the light of your own investing objectives:

(1) Some mutual funds invest in a broad spectrum of American industry, selecting bluest chip stocks in a spread of industries.

(2) Others choose the smaller stocks, hoping by means of diversification to lessen the risk inherent in the blue-sky approach while increasing profit potential from the portfolio components that happen to hit.

(3) Some are "balanced." These invest in bonds as well as stocks and tend to be more stable, except at times such as 1969, when both bond and stock markets were chaotic.

(4) Some funds invest in other funds. In practice these have usually proved no wiser than the average investor in choosing other funds. Investors who buy them add another layer of management costs and sometimes an added, although lower, load cost.

(5) Some funds are geographically oriented.

(6) There is one fund which sells shares only to members of the United States Armed Forces.

(7) Another invests only in letter stocks.

(8) Others slant their efforts to investment of venture capital in burgeoning enterprises. Risks are spread in this manner. A few big successes can swing the portfolio value sharply upward.

(9) There is a fund which invests in peace-oriented stocks.

(10) Another puts capital into companies which concentrate upon social issues.

(11) Still another devotes its efforts to dollar cost averaging—that statistical gimmick which fails to work about as often as it succeeds—in a set of forty stocks. This particular fund has made the technique work because it began in 1939 when stocks were starting a quarter-century of rising trend. Later, the manager admitted that "we have seventeen losers out of forty; the components for dollar averaging will have to be changed."

(12) One fund, sold in conjunction with an insurance policy, undertakes to guarantee holders against loss in asset value.

(13) The hedge-fund idea is still around. Whether it fares better in the future will depend upon how skillfully managements apply the technique. If you are interested in one of these

funds, look carefully at its record in good and bad markets, since according to the hedge theory the fund should profit from both trends.

Hedge funds were a development of the late sixties. They attempted to "hedge" against changing market conditions by always being short some stocks and long other stocks. In theory, the hedge concept had—and has—merit. But in practice among some mutual funds during troubled 1969 and 1970, the short positions were often in stocks going up while the fund owned stocks plummeting downward.

If a fund records financial rather than social prospects, make sure it fits your investing objective, then buy. If not, write a check as a contribution toward your favorite cause, but don't confuse investment with world betterment. Sound results will be achieved by appraisal of future trends and examination of past results and not by being doctrinaire about a cause, a technique, or a slant.

CRITERIA FOR CHOOSING A FUND

Look for the fund's statement of purpose. If your objective is capital gains and management tells you that the fund is seeking to develop a high, comfortable yield, give the rest of the prospectus a miss. If you want income, don't look farther than a fund statement that it seeks conservation of capital. This simple step, skipped by a majority of fund-buying investors, can spare an awful lot of non-achievement.

That's obvious and easy. Afterward, things get tougher.

Every analyst has his own ideas of how to judge a stock or a mutual fund. I look at the record. "Better to seek concepts," someone will counter. "Find a fund with a concept geared to the future."

I agree that a sound concept is essential but insist on examination of past performance because the past tells how well management was able to accomplish that objective named in the beginning of the prospectus. If the aim is to build capital and year by year the capital has built only slowly or not at all, there is reason to doubt the fund's chances of bringing off its aim in the future.

When the stated aim is high income and the current yield is 4 percent, that aim is being underachieved. This is especially true when, as I believe will be the case in coming years, competitive media such as bonds (we'll look at them and the yield power of mutual funds in the next chapter) pay better yields.

When the aim is capital conservation, look at the fund's past ability to counter inflation by producing a smidgin of increased capital value and a soupçon of increased yield. Without such a modest performance, the fund is losing out to inflation. (Warning: Look for only as much "growth" in a capital conservation fund as would keep up with the increase in groceries and apartment rentals.)

After examining the past as a means of judging a fund's management ability to bring off its aim in the future, then look at the concept. Social aims are as important as profit in corporate operation, and a fund which realizes that its component companies cannot go on generating profits while they generate air or water pollution is more likely to prove a winner in the period ahead.

Specialized funds can help at certain times because fashions in stocks change as do clothing styles. Funds geared to a fashion will prosper when the fad is in bloom and fade when their specialties no longer command Wall Street's favor.

Example: When the booming Japanese economy was in favor, shares of Japan Fund outperformed most investments. After imposition of the surtax in 1971, Japan Fund prices and performance reflected the prospect for an at least temporary slowdown.

Example: When gold stocks are in favor because conditions are such as to make knowledgeable people expect or fear a change in the price of the yellow metal, then shares of American–South African shoot up. (This is a closed-end fund which invests in South African securities, gold stocks prominent among them.)

Example: A worldwide energy shortage threatens. Certain mutual funds oriented toward energy stocks presumably should benefit.

Look for accumulated capital gains or losses in a fund's portfolio. The latest quarterly statement will list holdings from which this information can be extracted.

When a fund sells stocks at a profit, it generally passes these to its own shareholders in the form of special distributions which are classed as capital gains rather than ordinary income dividends. If you receive such a long-term capital gains dividend, it is treated for tax purposes as if you had held the stock yourself and realized a gain on the sale.

Generally, such distributions are paid out once a year, occasionally oftener. If you buy a fund immediately before the gains distribution you will pay on the basis of an asset value. This will almost immediately be paid back to you, *and you will be assessed a tax on it or what is, in effect, a return of part of your purchase money.* Better to buy after, rather than before, a capital gains distribution.

Sometimes, after a bear market appears to have bottomed, you can buy tax *credits.* Say your new fund has substantial tax losses from sales of portfolio components. If the fund later achieves capital gains, they can be offset against the previous tax losses. Explaining this in a memo to firm personnel, the head of mutual-fund sales of one large New York Stock Exchange member firm pointed out: "The potential value of realized and unrealized losses available to a fund portfolio manager affords a real or potential tax credit or tax shelter against which he can offset gains if he is successful in generating them. Instead of paying out realized gains to stockholders (thereby creating a taxable item for them and reducing the operating capital of the fund) he is able to retain the use of the money in his portfolio operation until such time as the *realized* gains offset the *realized* losses. This whole theme is predicated on the ability of a portfolio manager to perform well and generate gains."

Lesson: Buying stocks with tax credits is a wise idea.

When an industry swings into favor and there is a closed-end fund in the field, the closed end deserves special consideration if it is selling at a discount from asset value. If outside forces are such as to lift the fund to favor because of the area in which it operates or because it is in tune with special economic conditions, its discount can be replaced with a premium. Then two forces work to generate profits. The first is the expected rise (assuming your homework has been well done and the rise comes off) in underlying values of the fund's portfolio stocks. This increases net-asset value per share. Next, there is a gain in the vanishing of the discount and its replacement with a premium.

Judged in the light of information we have examined, mutual funds should be resultful investments in the decade ahead.

Chapter 5

INCOME AND GROWTH

For many years it was considered the purpose of investment to produce a steady if unspectacular yield in dividends or interest, while safeguarding the precious capital an investor had accumulated. Along came the growthomania of the sixties. The income approach was out.

"Dividends? Hell, I don't even know whether any of my stocks pay dividends," expounded one growth investor.

In the euphoria of the sixties, who indeed cared about how much an investment paid? It was how much it grew that mattered.

Then growth investments ungrew. Investors—those still possessing capital with which to try again—learned sadly that although growth was undependable, income could be counted on if an investor took care in choosing his vehicles, and that compounded income was able to produce a surer, if less enjoyable, way to make capital increase.

With the income approach, I'll grant that you won't have as much fun as you had picking little *wunderkinder* stocks, but you will probably be a lot richer by the 1980's.

We're going to look at:

(1) *Bonds,* those neglected, scoffed at, and scorned investments beloved of our financial ancestors and now fashionable again. Bonds are the IOU's of governments, companies, and others and come in many designations and styles.

(2) *Preferred stocks,* which are hybrid securities. Common stocks possess ownership privileges—at least in theory—and participate in the profits of a corporation. Bonds are debt instruments. Preferreds are a form of security—once popular, later neglected—which returned to the favor of issuing corporations arising from the merger madness of the sixties, when they furnished much of the so-called Chinese money with which conglomerates bought up control of smaller fish and even on occasion bigger fry than themselves. Under current and expected business/investment conditions, preferreds can have a special place for generating income.

(3) *Mutual funds* with good income records. Criteria for choosing these and guidelines for determining the place of mutuals in an income program will be considered.

(4) *Common stocks* are usually looked on as growth media. Many make superb income investments and have the ability— not shared by bonds and seldom by preferreds—of bringing about a gradual increase in the yield year by year. There is added risk in using common stocks for this purpose; risks and rewards will be examined and weighed. The extra risk comes about because high yields on common stocks sometimes come about when there is danger of the dividend being cut. Example: Say that Company A is earning only $2 but paying $2.50 in dividends. Unless the earnings grow spectacularly, the dividend must be cut—quickly turning the seemingly high yield into lower income.

(5) *Certificates of Deposit* are useful income generators in several ways. Their principal advantage is adaptability. They can be made to stretch over a number of investing problems in time and amount.

BONDS FOR BETTER DAYS

Of all vehicles used to generate investor income, bonds offer the widest possibilities. They come in more types than common stocks, pay more than banks or savings and loan deposits, and are more easily available to investors than some offboard equities. At certain times and under certain economic conditions, bonds have brought in spectacular capital gains as well.

Bonds are issued when a borrowing entity needs to raise money. They offer some advantages over stock to the seller. Ownership isn't watered as it would be when one million shares are added to an existing supply of five million shares, with the result that each share's proportionate equity in the corporation, and absolute portion of profit, is lessened. A company does not have to pay dividends on its stock; many high-grade companies do not, or else pay only a small amount to stockholders. But a company does have to pay the stipulated interest on its bonds unless it wants to have its credit wrecked and its future ability to raise funds seriously impaired. Bond interest is a fixed cost. It is paid before computation of income taxes. Thus a company's payout for interest is lessened by the amount it would have had to pay in state, federal, and sometimes local levies on income if the fixed-cost item of interest had not existed. Dividends are different. Since they are a payout of a part of net profit, they come after computation of income tax and in no real sense lessen the amount due the tax collector.

In theory at least—this is difficult to enforce in any real situation—bondholders have the right to demand liquidation of a company when it cannot pay them. This doesn't apply in all cases, but is true in a sufficient percentage to consider it a rough rule. Stockholders own a company; bondholders are its creditors.

Some bonds are mortgage bonds. These are secured by land, buildings, or other property. Other bonds are backed by dedication of specific kinds of income to paying their interest and furnishing a fund for orderly retirement when the bonds come due. Bonds unsecured by such theoretical protections are called debentures. It would seem that a mortgage bond should be safer than an income bond and that both would be safer than a debenture. In practice things don't work that way. The debenture of a high-grade company with the means to pay its debts and the habit of doing so are usually a safer play than even mortgage bonds of a less solid venture.

It is easier to judge the merits of a bond than of a stock. All you have to do is check the ratings. Bond ratings are sometimes

inaccurate, but they are the only guide an investor has. Moreover, despite an occasional spectacular failure of judgment such
as happened with Penn Central, bond ratings are usually sound
and nearly always valuable.

Ratings are issued by two services, Standard & Poor's and
Moody's, and are available from any brokerage firm. They range,
in descending order of quality, from AAA to lower alphabetical
combinations. Ratings apply to many types of bonds, classified
usually by the kind of issuer, and are then graded according to
methods of the bond-rating statistical firms. The one exception
applies to bonds of the United States government. In addition to
the familiar savings bonds sold by payroll deduction and adver-
tised on television as a patriotic duty and a way to grow steadily
rich, government debt instruments, sometimes called Treasuries,
come in *bonds, notes,* and *bills.*

Bonds are the Treasuries of long-term maturity. Notes come
next, and bills are obligations of short-term (some three months)
maturity. The latter have a special applicability which we will
consider in chapter 9.

Savings bonds are sold in amounts of small face value, but
marketable Treasuries come in $1,000 and larger denominations.
They are bought and sold in the same way you would purchase
or dispose of common stocks. Some corporate bonds, which also
generally come in $1,000 denominations, are traded on the New
York Stock Exchange or its small cousin, the American. Most
savings bonds—and all Treasuries—are traded over-the-counter.
You can read current bond quotations in the daily papers that
carry stock quotations.

Interest yields are determined partly by the money market
which sets going rates of return, and partly by the ratings of
the bonds. The rule of thumb is: the bigger the yield, the greater
the risk; smaller yield, lesser risk. Government bonds usually pay
less in percentage return than bonds of any other class because
it is considered unthinkable that either interest or eventual repayment of the principal amount should be skipped. The United
States government in the past has defaulted on its word, both
written and spoken by its highest officials; it has broken treaties;
paid debts incurred in gold by using currency of quality not com-
parable to gold; issued gold and silver certificates and replaced

them with notes of Federal Reserve debt; and removed the silver content from coins and replaced it with copper. It has done all manner of things which at an earlier time it promised not to do. But it has never skipped payment of either principal or interest on its bonds.

In this respect the federal government is like a fight-racket figure of an earlier day, known as the Honest Brakeman. A newspaperman inquired of one fight manager the reason for his name. "Why, he never stole a freight car," replied the manager.

Next in quality, and often equal to corporates in yield, are the bonds of government agencies, such as the Home Loan Bank. The Federal National Mortgage Association ("Fannie Mae" from the sound of its initials) and the Government National Mortgage Association ("Ginny Mae") are others of the bond-issuing semi-autonomous agencies proliferated by our welfare state. The interest and principal repayment on these, although theoretically a little less safe than direct debts of the federal establishment, are in practice as safe as the income and principal of Treasury bonds. Neither a Republican nor Democratic administration could permit semi-government bonds to go into default.

Corporate bonds are issued by companies as diverse in size and stability as General Motors Corp. and General Wingding Industries, which operates out of Joe Glotz' garage. In this area, careful examination of the alphabetical designations of rating services can save a bond buyer future grief.

Generally, bonds of a given quality rating will sell at approximately the same yield, which is not to say that they will sell at the same price.

Yield is percentage of return. If a bond yields 6 percent, it might be an older 3 percent bond—there are many of these in existence—which sells around $50 in order to pay 6 percent. Or it might be a new 6 percent instrument selling at par, or $100. Bond prices are quoted with $100 as par, but since a majority of bonds have $1,000 denominations, this means that $1,000 represents $100 and the 6 percent bond at par will cost $1,000, with the 3 percent bond quoted at $50 selling around $500.

The 3 percent instrument is a "discount" bond. It offers special opportunity. Part of the yield represents eventual profit on a bond bought below par and redeemed on maturity at full

$1,000. Thus the bond would be selling around—not at—$500, since the per-year built-in profit would depend upon the number of years until maturity. Example: If the bond had a 10-year-away maturity, its annual accrual of gain, in addition to interest, would come to $50. If it had only five years to go until maturity, the accrual would come to $100 in addition to interest payment. Assuming eventual redemption at full par on maturity, the accrual would represent (under tax laws prevailing as this is written) a capital gain taxable at a lower rate than the amount received in ordinary interest.

And the possibility exists that going interest rates will descend to a point where prime and the yield on other topgrade bonds would be smaller than prevailing 6 percent rates which we considered. Should that occur, the discount bond would rise in price to a point where its yield to maturity would be roughly equal to that of other bonds of the same grade.

The 6 percent bond selling at full par when rates are 6 percent would also rise *but not to as great a degree*. The reason is that, once the 6 percent bond rose over par, it would offer a built-in *loss* to maturity which would have to be considered in appraising its true yield. Thus it is easier for a bond bought at discount when things were tight to rise toward par than it is for a high-coupon bond purchased at par to rise an equal amount over redemption price.

Some corporate bonds are convertible. (So are some preferred stocks, a class of income investment which we will examine shortly.) This means that at the bond owner's option he can convert his evidences of a corporation's debt into shares of its common-stock ownership. If a company has lively prospects, this is a kicker that can add to the attraction of the bond investment since, when the common goes up, the bondholder is able to switch into the common and take a resulting capital gain.

The "Personal Business" section of *Business Week*'s September 26, 1970, issue explained how to appraise the investment worth of a convertible bond: "You will first want to figure a convertible's value solely as a bond. For this have your broker check investment value ratings that show what the bond's current price would be without a conversion feature. Rule of thumb: If a convertible is selling for more than 25 percent to 35 percent over this value, you might be assuming about as much risk as you would in buying the common stock itself. Even here, though, there would still be some advantage: A convertible usually will fall only as low as its estimated investment value."

That's a good rule for convertible investment appraisal if you also keep in mind that "investment value" fluctuates. It will depend upon going rates of interest. We have seen how a bond can be issued at 3 percent during easy-money days when that is the low prevailing interest, and then later drop to around half its starting price should the rate of interest double. This doubling of interest rates, and consequent near-halving of bond prices, even on topnotch IOU's, occurred during a short five-year period after 1966.

In appraising probable values on convertibles or straight bonds, you cannot ignore the swings of interest rates unless your bond is bought to hold until maturity.

One class of bond has the ability to shelter income yield from federal taxation and, depending upon state laws, occasionally from state income taxes as well. These are called municipals. They embrace the debt obligations of states, counties, cities, towns, villages, special taxing units such as school boards, toll roads, and other district authorities.

The quality of municipals varies as does the quality of corporation bonds. Like corporates, municipals are rated on an alphabetical scale by the services which appraise financial standing. With some municipals, both interest payment and sinking-fund provisions to ultimately pay them off on maturity are dependent upon income from, for example, a toll bridge. Trouble can ensue if that income proves inadequate to service the bonds. In practice the issuing authority usually dedicates other income to the bonds rather than see its credit rating slip. In my home area, tolls from a long causeway were inadequate to pay off bonds issued to build the structure. The state then dedicated revenues from some auto license fees as an alternative to costly default on the bonds. But you can't count on this happening.

Safer bonds are those backed by "the full faith and credit" of a state, county, or municipality. When this provision applies, then the total taxing authority, including raising property taxes at need, is behind the bond.

Municipals, again like corporation bonds, sell at different yields depending upon the rating. A highly rated bond offers a lower return than a risky revenue bond of an authority organized to throw a toll bridge across a swamp where nobody wants to go. Whether highly rated or not, a municipal will sell at a lower return on the invested dollar than a corporate bond of equal quality rating. The reason is the tax-free status of return an investor receives.

No investor should rush to buy municipals just because of the tax-free feature. Determine first whether the municipal furnishes the best net return on your tax bracket. Say you are in a 20 percent tax bracket. An A-rated corporate bond pays 7 percent, an A-rated municipal 5 percent. After taxes, you would have 5.6 percent yield on the corporate bond, compared to the net 5 percent yield on the tax-exempt municipal. Municipals aren't always cheap; buy them only if you are in a sufficiently high bracket for the saving to be real instead of seeming.

Example: Say that an investor is in a 40 percent tax bracket. A taxable bond yields him 6 percent. After paying the income tax on the interest, he will have only 3.6 percent net return. A tax-exempt bond pays 4 percent but he keeps it all. Under those circumstances, return on the tax-exempt bond is actually higher.

An important bond consideration is whether to buy one with early or far-off maturity. When you are worried that future money conditions might make bonds go down (when interest yields go up, the prices of older bonds slide), then it's best to purchase early maturity. You can count upon a payoff soon without loss and a profit if the bond is purchased at discount.

If your aim, on the other hand, is to secure high interest yield over a long period of time, then buy the bond with far-off maturity. Make certain, however, that it has no call clause. A call clause permits the issuer to call in a bond for redemption before the date of maturity. The main reason for call clauses is that they permit the issuer to get rid of his high interest debt during times of easier money. Sometimes a call date is so far away that for shorter-term purposes it might as well not exist. Sometimes it is an advantage, because if the bond is called (provided it is a low coupon bond at discount from par), your profit would be immediately achieved.

PREFERRED STOCKS

Few investors know much about preferred stocks. In an informative booklet, the investment firm of Halsey, Stuart and Co., Inc., pointed out:

> Preferred stocks occupy a unique position in the structure of investment securities. Legally, preferred stock represents an equity or ownership interest in a corporation. However, because of the contractual nature of preferred stock, in the payment of dividends the preferred holder is at times afforded the preferential treatment of a creditor rather than that of an equity owner. Preferred stocks offer the advantages of stable revenue and security of principal. Preferred stock usually does not have voting rights and holders cannot therefore elect directors. However, as a rule, preferreds have contingent voting rights —they can elect some directors in times of financial trouble.

Until the wave of mergers in the late 1960's, the use of preferred stocks in corporate finance had dropped off sharply, mainly because of the high after-tax cost of the dividend to the issuer. Since the interest paid on debt is deductible in computing the issuing company's Federal income tax and other income taxes, a dividend paid on a preferred issue (which is not tax-deductible) costs the company almost twice as much as a like amount of interest on debt.

Another reason for the sharp decline in preferred stock issues relates to the hybrid nature of preferred stock. From the point of view of the investor, a preferred stock does not endow the investor with the strong and enforceable rights of a creditor. Preferred dividends are subordinated to bond interest and to taxes, and are subject to suspension under circumstances which would not rule out the payment of bond interest. Regular dividend payments depend entirely upon the vote of the Board of Directors, which can withhold dividends in its discretion if deemed advisable (the Directors may wish to retain cash for expansion of emergency reserves). It should be noted that some preferreds are "cumulative"— if a dividend is omitted, it accumulates and is paid with future dividend payments. At the same time, preferred stock to some extent denies the holder the opportunity of sharing in the future growth of the company. Thus, while preferred stockholders contribute to the financial strength and security of the company, they suffer the greatest from financial misfortunes that may arise. However, in many cases these contractual shortcomings can be overcome by the strength of the issuer. If issued by a financially strong corporation a preferred stock can represent a sound investment.

Thus preferreds can be worthwhile income investments when (1) issued by companies of sufficient soundness and stability to make the continuance of dividends appear after careful appraisal to be at least as secure as continuance of bond interest; (2) the yield is high; and (3) there is a convertible feature which adds to the attraction without subtracting from the yield factor for which the convertible is purchased.

MUTUAL FUNDS

"Why?" an investor asked me when I suggested certain mutual funds to fulfill his income needs. "Aren't mutual funds designed to be capital gains vehicles?"

Not all are designed for that function. Some are set up to furnish income. Usually, their yields are smaller than might be obtained on bonds or preferreds. Which brings another question: Why take a smaller yield, then pay a loading charge in some cases and a management fee in all cases when you can have a higher yield buying bonds and some preferreds?

Investing isn't a solely today process. It should look toward tomorrow as well. The record of income-oriented mutual funds shows that many of them have been able to generate small but worthwhile growth in income by slanting some of their investments toward companies that possess prospects of paying bigger dividends in future than at present. The yield of 4.5 percent today might become 5 percent next year, 6.5 two years hence, and as high as 9 percent a decade away, so that the total income return over a long term is greater than would be obtainable from investments of fixed yield, such as bonds and preferreds.

One income fund said of its modus operandi: "The Fund is primarily designed to emphasize current income with a secondary, but nonetheless important, objective of obtaining capital appreciation consistent with the Fund's primary objective, and both consistent with the preservation of capital. The Fund will attempt to achieve its objectives principally by investing in fixed income securities, a substantial portion of which may also have a call on the common stock through a conversion privilege or by attached warrants and, secondarily, by investing in common stocks which offer attractive current dividend yields with potential for capital appreciation."

COMMON STOCKS

The prospectus quoted above outlined one of the reasons for using common stocks as growth vehicles along with bonds, preferreds, and some mutuals. Wisely chosen stocks have the promise of increasing dividends so that income at least maintains pace with inflation.

Yields of 10 to 12 percent are sometimes available in common stocks. Wary old birds shy away from such high yields. High yield in a common stock is sometimes the sign of a bargain, more often a warning of danger. The prospects for the company are such that its product is in danger of growing obsolescent, its profit about to halve, and competition in its fields becoming tighter. "A 10 percent yield usually becomes a 5 percent return within a few months," one old hand told me. He was right. When you see an exceptionally high common-stock yield, investigate before rushing to buy.

CERTIFICATES OF DEPOSIT

These lend-us-now-we'll-pay-you-later instruments of banks have the happy faculty of adaptability. They can be tailored for length of maturity and yield. In the chapter on investing for the short term (Chapter 9), we will examine in detail how Certificates of Deposit (CD's) are employed for short-term investment purposes. That does not mean that CD's lack attraction for the long term as well.

TABLE 5. AMOUNT OF $1 AT COMPOUND
INTEREST

Number of years	4.1%	4.6%	5.1%	5.6%	6.1%	6.6%	7.1%	7.6%
1	1.04100	1.04600	1.05100	1.05600	1.06100	1.06600	1.07100	1.07600
2	1.08368	1.09411	1.10460	1.11513	1.12572	1.13635	1.14704	1.15777
3	1.12811	1.14444	1.16093	1.17758	1.19438	1.21135	1.22848	1.24576
4	1.17436	1.19708	1.22014	1.24352	1.26724	1.29130	1.31570	1.34044
5	1.22251	1.25215	1.28236	1.31316	1.34454	1.37653	1.40911	1.44231
6	1.27263	1.30975	1.34776	1.38670	1.42656	1.46738	1.50916	1.55193
7	1.32481	1.37000	1.41650	1.46435	1.51358	1.56422	1.61631	1.66987
8	1.37912	1.43302	1.48874	1.54635	1.60591	1.66746	1.73107	1.79678
9	1.43567	1.49894	1.56467	1.63295	1.70387	1.77751	1.85397	1.93334
10	1.49453	1.56789	1.64447	1.72440	1.80780	1.89483	1.98560	2.08027
11	1.55580	1.64001	1.72833	1.82096	1.91808	2.01989	2.12658	2.23837
12	1.61959	1.71545	1.81648	1.92294	2.03508	2.15320	2.27757	2.40849
13	1.68599	1.79436	1.90912	2.03062	2.15922	2.29531	2.43928	2.59154
14	1.75512	1.87690	2.00648	2.14433	2.29094	2.44680	2.61246	2.78849
15	1.82708	1.96324	2.10881	2.26442	2.43068	2.60829	2.79795	3.00042
16	1.90199	2.05355	2.21636	2.39122	2.57895	2.78044	2.99660	3.22845
17	1.97997	2.14801	2.32940	2.52513	2.73627	2.96394	3.20936	3.47381
18	2.06115	2.24682	2.44819	2.66654	2.90318	3.15956	3.43723	3.73782
19	2.14566	2.35017	2.57305	2.81586	3.08028	3.36810	3.68127	4.02190
20	2.23363	2.45828	2.70428	2.97355	3.26817	3.59039	3.94264	4.32756
21	2.32521	2.57136	2.84220	3.14007	3.46753	3.82736	4.22257	4.65645
22	2.42054	2.68964	2.98715	3.31591	3.67905	4.07996	4.52237	5.01034
23	2.51978	2.81336	3.13949	3.50161	3.90347	4.34924	4.84346	5.39113
24	2.62309	2.94278	3.29961	3.69770	4.14158	4.63629	5.18734	5.80086
25	2.73064	3.07815	3.46789	3.90477	4.39422	4.94228	5.55564	6.24172
26	2.84259	3.21974	3.64475	4.12343	4.66227	5.26847	5.95009	6.71609
27	2.95914	3.36785	3.83063	4.35435	4.94666	5.61619	6.37255	7.22651
28	3.08046	3.52277	4.02599	4.59819	5.24841	5.98686	6.82500	7.77573
29	3.20676	3.68482	4.23132	4.85569	5.56856	6.38199	7.30958	8.36668
30	3.33824	3.85432	4.44711	5.12760	5.90825	6.80320	7.82856	9.00255
31	3.47511	4.03162	4.67392	5.41475	6.26865	7.25221	8.38438	9.68675
32	3.61759	4.21707	4.91229	5.71798	6.65104	7.73086	8.97968	10.4229
33	3.76591	4.41105	5.16281	6.03818	7.05675	8.24109	9.61723	11.2150
34	3.92031	4.61396	5.42611	6.37632	7.48721	8.78501	10.3000	12.0674
35	4.08104	4.82620	5.70285	6.73339	7.94393	9.36482	11.0313	12.9845
36	4.24836	5.04821	5.99369	7.11046	8.42851	9.98289	11.8145	13.9713
37	4.42255	5.28043	6.29937	7.50865	8.94265	10.6417	12.6534	15.0331
38	4.60387	5.52333	6.62064	7.92913	9.48815	11.3441	13.5518	16.1757
39	4.79263	5.77740	6.95829	8.37317	10.0669	12.0928	14.5139	17.4050
40	4.98913	6.04316	7.31316	8.84206	10.6810	12.8909	15.5444	18.7278

Interest rates on other instruments often turn down before banks begin to shave the yields they pay on CD's. At such times, even longer-term Certificates possess important merit. On most occasions, however, their virtues lie in short-view investing.

PLOWBACK—THE ROAD TO CAPITAL BUILDING

Plowback is the technique, discussed briefly in Chapter 3, for making an income investment bring about capital growth by putting back all income into new bonds and more shares of preferred or common, in order to produce still higher income tomorrow which can be plowed back into still more bonds or stock to produce even greater income the day after tomorrow and increased capital value thereafter. Ad infinitum.

Table 5 was compiled by Union Carbide Company. It indicates the extent to which $1 of investment will increase in any given number of years if plowed back (compounded) to become investment capital.

Chapter 6

HOW TO FIND
GOOD INVESTMENT ADVICE

In the middle of 1971, a financial paper made a survey of the opinions of people who set up as stock-market specialists. A majority were sure that stocks would go nowhere but upward the rest of the year. The Dow Jones Industrial Average was at 900 when all this hot wind was being blown around the financial district. The market was down below 800 five months later. How could all the experts blow it?

THE SOURCES OF INVESTMENT ADVICE

Although the goofs and gaffs of experts stand out for all to see, there *is* sound advice to be had if you know how to judge it, when to ignore it, and whom to seek for help. This chapter will tell you how to find the minority of advisers worth heeding and ways to determine whether they're speaking wisely or have lost touch with reality.

Brokers Most people turn to a broker. The man who gives them buy and sell advice is typically a registered representative who occupies a desk in one of the hundreds of board rooms that dot the country. He may merely pass along suggestions from his firm's research department, which might consist of a vice-president and a secretary occupying broom-closet quarters littered with statistical studies and wastepaper, or might consist of hundreds of people working over a full floor and more, in downtown Manhattan. Or the registered rep may advise customers out of his own wisdom, based upon observation of the tape and/or tips received from other customers. You can't tell the worth of advice from its source because many reps possess intelligence or fact sources superior to the facilities of their firms' financial analyst staffs.

Recommendations from brokerage-house research staffs are usually well grounded. However, many of the facts so minutely assembled have little bearing on the investment merits of a situation. They're told everything including the color of paint in the executive men's rooms. Most of the facts have about as much to do with the stock as a study of the phases of the moon.

That proliferation of minute detail is one drawback of brokerage-house investment studies. Another drawback is the widespread dissemination of brokerage recommendations. The bigger the brokerage house, the greater the number of investors who become exposed to research's latest hot lead. When a sufficient number of people, representing a sizable block of stock-buying dollars, is exposed to a recommendation and acts upon it, the recommendation becomes self-defeating.

Example: American Mugwump is trading at 30. The research department of Blunder, Brilliant, Mournful and Gay has studied the Mugwump situation and decided that its prospects in the coming market phase are very good. A research report is prepared and put on the customer reading racks the length and width of North America. Many read it. Hundreds rush to the desks of their registered reps to put in buy orders on American Mugwump, ranging from 50 to 500 shares. These orders represent a large amount of money flowing across the specialist's order book over a short period of time. The price of American Mugwump is marked up to 36. To fill orders, the specialist sells short a block of the stock.

Whenever a specialist has a large short position of his own, there is strong probability that the stock's price will sink. New York Stock Exchange propaganda to the contrary, specialists do have the power to control short-term movements of the stocks they supposedly only stabilize. Within a week or ten days, the price of American Mugwump, with the force of recommended buying spent and the force of specialist manipulation going against it, is back at 30. The investors who bought at the beginning price of 30 are even. Those who bought later have losses. The ones who read the recommendation of Blunder, Brilliant, Mournful and Gay late and purchased part of the specialist's short-sale block at 36 have a considerable loss. (When the specialist "sells short," he sells stocks which he does not possess, expecting to buy in the stocks later on when the price of the security has declined. He is compelled to sell short when there is no other way to furnish stock that public investors want to buy. By doing so, he usually "cleans up" all outstanding buy orders and is then able to expect eventual profit, since he knows that the buying surge has been exhausted.)

No matter how sincerely it is meant and without regard to the care with which a firm guards against too-early disclosure of the recommendation, *any recommendation which is widely disseminated tends to be self-defeating.* This holds true not only for recommendations made to big numbers of investors by brokerage firms, but equally for recommendations of independent research and advisory services whose recommendations reach a widespread investor audience.

Thus many brokerage reports are well-researched, intelligently interpreted, carefully considered—and achieve nothing except to generate commissions for the firms that put them out. Many registered representatives of big investment houses know this. "Don't ask me for our research people's suggestions," one broker said. "Everybody reads them. They're as bland as corn flakes. Now *I* have some ideas the research staff doesn't know and mine won't get acted on by everybody. Just the other day I was talking to a customer whose brother-in-law is related by marriage to the husband of the cleaning woman who empties wastebaskets in the office of the president of American Mugwump, and he says . . ."

Many registered reps' recommendations are about as soundly based as that. Endlessly searching for something to recommend to customers and aware that without recommendations to stimulate buying, commissions can dry up, brokers for individuals tend to grasp at such informational straws as that fed to an investor by a rep in the hometown office of Blunder, Brilliant, Mournful and Gay. Not all reps' ideas are farfetched, however.

Most brokers are men tied to the tape that unwinds across a screen on the front wall, and umbilicaled to a telephone wire. Receiving investment advice from them is a little like asking the druggist instead of the doctor to diagnose and prescribe for an ache. It may work, but odds are against it. However, some reps are shrewder judges of market trends and of investment values than the financial analysts who staff their companies' research departments.

I don't like the broker as a source for investment ideas, but I'd take the suggestions of a really sound rep before heeding those disseminated to a continent by the firm's research reports.

Professional Counselors Professional counselors guide many investors' decisions. These men are the doctors of the money trade. The medical profession has a rather high level of average competence. Not so the investment counseling profession. Thirty percent of the practitioners of investment counseling are incompetent, 60 percent mediocre—in the sense that given a big bull market they will achieve close-to-average results, with close-to-average losses during the downturns they seldom foresee and rarely cope with—and only 10 percent possess really high abilities. That poor showing is better than the showing of the brokerage fraternity. Shortly, we'll examine criteria for determining whether a counselor who has solicited your account should be ranked among the thirty miserables, the sixty moderately competents, or the ten whizzes.

Not all counselors will take small investment accounts. Their service is on a highly personal basis, advising each client in the light of his needs and wants as well as his means. With service so personal and the tie-up of time and effort for each client high, there is need to make the service bring in high fees. Fees are generally set as a percentage of the amount to be managed by the counselor. A typical fee might run to two percent per year of invested portfolio value on the first $100,000 and one

percent or one-half of one percent on amounts above that. A
minimum fee often restricts the service to those possessing
$50,000 or $100,000 funds to be invested.

Some investment counselors accept smaller clients—including
accounts as relatively small as $5,000—for group handling. Under
such a plan, a client, although probably holding his own securi
ties or having them in the custody of his own brokerage firm
becomes part of a group. All members of the group, chosen for
homogeneity of interests, needs, and aims, receive identical
recommendations at the same time.

Market Letters   Market letters guide many. A drawback
to much market-letter information is the same as that which ap
plies to brokerage-house reports. If a big firm issues the recom
mendation, it is likely to bring about a temporary rise and almost
immediate slump in price exactly as in the case of Blunder
Brilliant, Mournful and Gay's suggestion that investors buy
American Mugwump common. In general, the recommendation
of the big services tend to be most valuable in the area of indus
try studies ("The market for mugwumps should be good within
the foreseeable future and all companies in the industry can
prosper" . . . "We think auto sales will slump in the year ahead
and recommend selling auto stocks") or studies of overall market
direction. The worth of any recommendation is not to be judged
by the price paid to subscribe to the service or the size of th
organization issuing the recommendation.

The writers of market letters tend to be less staid and pro
fessorial in manner than counselors who aid affluent accounts
but the percentages of poor, merely able, and brilliant practition
ers is about the same as that of the counseling group.

Tipsters   The neighborhood tipster is a more poten
source of advice than professionals believe. "Hey, did you hear
that Sam who lives down the street made a bundle in American
Mugwump?" is a kind of word that spreads from backdoor to
telephone to downtown coffeehouse, and at all levels exerts great
influence.

The breakdown for neighborly investment advice would show
that 90 percent is probably misinformed and misguided, 3 per
cent malicious, and 7 percent bland rehashes of long-known ma
terial.

Joe the backfence tipster is the most expensive investment guide you can find.

ALL ADVISERS HAVE CERTAIN WEAKNESSES

Ethical Standards Ethical standards of a great portion of the advisory group are very high. But like plumbers, house-painters, doctors, and lawyers, the advisory fraternity has its share of those who step over the boundaries. The following paragraphs were taken from the *News Digest* of the Securities and Exchange Commission during a single month:

SEC News Digest, Nov. 8, 1971:

The SEC has issued an order suspending Analytical Investment Decision Systems, Inc., d/b/a AIDS, of Bellevue, Wash., an applicant for registration as an investment adviser, and Robert E. Bronson III, its president and a director, and Virgil A. Counter, a director, from engaging in the investment advisory business for 30 days. The order made the suspension and registration application effective upon its issuance.

The suspension was based on findings that from January through April 1971, respondents among other things engaged in the investment advisory business without registration and violated antifraud provisions of the securities laws in that they directly and indirectly published and distributed advertisements which contained prohibited testimonials concerning AIDS' services, referred to past specific securities recommendations without furnishing required information as to each such recommendation, and used bait advertising techniques. In addition, according to the Commission's decision, respondents made misleading statements concerning the advisory services to be rendered by the firm.

The Commission's action was taken pursuant to an offer of settlement filed by respondents in which, without admitting or denying the charges, they consented to the above findings and the indicated sanctions, and the firm agreed to make restitution of all fees paid by clients during the period in question.

SEC News Digest, Nov. 9, 1971:

> The Commission has ordered administrative proceed
> ings under the Securities Exchange Act against the fol
> lowing: Capital Counsellors, Inc., registered broker
> dealer of New York, Capital Advisors, Inc., registered in
> vestment adviser of New York, J. Irving Weiss, presiden
> of both firms, Abraham B. Weiss, vice president of both
> firms, William Swedlow, Anne Purvin, Sherman Bush
> and Arthur Bernhardt who were employed by Counsel
> lors and Advisers during the period in question.
>
> The Commission's Division of Trading and Markets
> alleges, among other things, that during the period from
> January 1968 to March 1971, some or all of the respond
> ents offered and sold securities, namely the Bond Plan
> an investment contract, when no registration statemen
> was filed or in effect as to such securities, gave false and
> misleading information to the Commission to obtain a
> "no-action" letter for the sale by Counsellors and Ad
> visors of Counsellors' Bond Plan without registration
> disseminated advertisements which referred, directly o
> indirectly, to testimonials concerning the advice, analysis
> reports, and other circumstances rendered, and hypothe
> cated, arranged for and permitted the continued hypothe
> cation of securities carried for the accounts of customer
> under circumstances in which securities carried for the
> accounts of customers were hypothecated and subjec
> to liens of pledges for a sum in excess of the aggregate
> indebtedness of all customers in respect of such securi
> ties.

SEC News Digest, Nov. 12, 1971:

> The Commission announced the filing of a complaint
> yesterday in Federal district court in New York against
> forty-four defendants based on allegations of one or more
> anti-fraud provisions of the Federal securities laws in
> cluding the Investment Advisers Act of 1940. In addi
> tion, the complaint also alleges that certain of the de
> fendants violated various provisions of the Investment
> Company Act by conduct including one or more of the

following matters: the acceptance of compensation other than regular salary and wages by a person associated with registered investment companies for the purchase and sale of property to or for such investment companies; and gross misconduct and gross abuse of trust with respect to investment companies managed by certain of the defendants. The complaint based on all of the foregoing alleged violations seeks injunctive relief against the named defendants.

Named as defendants in the complaint are the following persons: Everest Management Corporation, New York; John Peter Galanis, New York; Akiyoshi Yamada, New York; Takara Asset Management Corp., New York; Louis G. Zachary, Summit, N.J.; Anthony M. Pilaro, New York; Armstrong Investors S.A., Nassau, Bahamas; Armstrong Capital S.A., Nassau, Bahamas; First National City Trust Company, Nassau, Bahamas; Howard Lawrence, Nassau, Bahamas; Meridian Capital Corporation, Hillsborough, Calif.; Robert R. Hagopian, Hillsborough, Calif.; Winfield & Co., Inc., San Mateo, Calif.; Winfield Associates, Inc., San Mateo, Calif.; Haywood Management Corporation, New York; A. S. Stephen Sanders, New York; Summit Group, Inc., Houston; Charles E. Hurwitz, Houston; F. Peter Zoch, III, New York; IRI Management Corp., New York; Jay H. Zises, Forest Hills, N.Y.; Paul R. Dupee, Jr., New York; Mates Management Company, Inc., New York; Frederic S. Mates, New York; Jerome E. Treisman, New York; James F. Khawly, Miami; George C. Van Aken, Cove Neck, L.I., N.Y.; Ramon N. D'Onofrio, New York; Alfred P. Herbert, Zurich, Switzerland; Bank Hoffman A.G., Zurich, Switzerland; Morton S. Kaplan, Miami Beach, Fla.; Robert S. Persky, New York; Microthermal Applications, Inc., Bellevue, Wash.; Nationwide Marketing Associates, Inc., Miami; Richard J. Kirschbaum, Oyster Bay, N.Y.; Charles J. Fischer, Short Hills, N.J.; Jerome E. Silverman, New York; Philip Zane, Jericho, N.Y.; United States Secretarial Institute, Ltd., Merrick, N.Y.; Laventhol, Krekstein, Horwath, East

Brunswick, N.J.; Morton Dear, East Brunswick, N.J.; Robert E. Bier, East Brunswick, N.J.; Thomas Martino, Jr., East Brunswick, N.J.; and Ira N. Smith, New York.

Influence of Commissions   The man or firm that advises investors might have commissions uppermost in mind over client service. This is particularly true when an adviser is also a broker. It is difficult for one whose livelihood is dependent upon buy and sell orders, and who has the power to generate such orders by a recommendation, to refrain from such recommendations.

Independent counselors unconnected with brokerage firms are not exempt from this temptation. When they hold clients' limited powers-of-attorney to put in orders through a single brokerage firm, it becomes tempting to generate orders so as to attain personal preference in the house—and sometimes for the sake of bribes paid to make commissionable business.

Follow-the-Leader Advice   A follow-the-leader mentality among advisers is not deliberate and probably operates in similar fields. Service A recommends a stock. It goes up. Clients of Service B write to the publisher to ask why he wasn't smart like the people who run Service A. He could reply that this was the first correct thing the analysts at A have done in a year. If he is smart, he does not. Next time, he avoids criticism by quickly looking into situations recommended by other services and, since he starts with a conclusion half formed, is likely to arrive at the same recommendation-to-buy made by Service A. It may not be good analytical technique, but it keeps advisers out of client trouble.

Another cause of simultaneous recommendations is the omnipresent computer. Since the same facts are available to all, it is not surprising that computers tend to come up with the same buy and sell signals at the same time. If everyone acts together, then everything stagnates.

Investment Philosophy   Many advisers possess a "philosophy" of investment. They may be growth-stock specialists, or bond men, or married to the idea that 1932 is around every corner and the correct investment procedure is therefore one of extreme caution. Any philosophy has to be wrong a great deal of the time.

During the troubled fall days that closed 1971, I received a letter from an investor asking what philosophy I favored.

"None," I told him.

A philosophy is good for philosophers. It's well for politicians to have basic philosophies to guide them. In this field the only workable philosophy is to have an aim of (1) preserving capital from loss and (2) making it bring a good return, which can be either dividends and interest or capital gain. A broad approach like that means that you embrace the philosophy of selling short and other bear market tactics when the trend is down, and that you flex the philosophy to different techniques when the bear wind ceases to blow.

If you can find an adviser who has flexibility, you will have secured an able source of counseling.

Bland Advice Bland and bullish are adjectives that fit many advisers. Because people congenitally hate a boat-rocker, advisers tend to tell bland news and to hold bland views which will not disturb their clients or cause the clients to think unhappy thoughts. Most investors prefer to hear a projection of better times and higher stock prices; therefore advisers tend to be bullish even at times that justify extreme bearishness.

I know from experience in publishing a market letter that clientele falls off by as much as one-third as soon as I air a bearish view and advise that stocks and mutual funds be sold. Being correct is no defense against the fallout in subscriptions and fees. People like to hear happy news, and therefore a large number of professional advisers furnish what is wanted.

CRITERIA FOR SELECTING AN INVESTMENT ADVISER

(1) Broker, counselor, newsletter, or neighborhood tipster? All except the latter have something to recommend them. The broker is "free" in that he does not assess a fee atop his commissions. If he is inept, he will cost more than a counselor might charge. If he is commission-minded, he might churn the account to develop charges. An adviser should be chosen more for ability than for

the classification into which he falls. I believe the professiona
counselor or the writer of letter advice tends to be better; he ha:
no stock in the firm's inventory which he is expected to push anc
won't—if he is honest—gain from commission generation. H
has time to analyze stocks and situations.

(2) What is his record? This is the most important piece o
information you can use in judging an adviser, and this is para
doxically the most difficult to obtain.

The Securities and Exchange Commission and state regulatory
bodies insist that an adviser must show all recommendations ove
the course of a year and cannot merely state, "I'm the man wh
recommended American Mugwump at ten before it rose to forty.
He may have been wrong on two other recommendations; th
SEC rules make sure he divulges that fact. In doing so, the rule:
unwittingly make for investor confusion because the recom
mendation which led to a thirty-point gain overshadows tw
which might have resulted in three-point losses each. A mer
listing of recommendations can confuse; examine it carefully t
determine not only the number of right and wrong recommenda
tions but also the degree to which each was right. If an inves101
had put an equal dollar amount into each suggestion, how woulc
he have fared?

The counselors who guide individual accounts guard identi
ties of their accounts and are acting in good ethics when they dc
so. Not only are a client's financial affairs confidential, but hi:
identity and the fact that he has financial affairs at all should no
be divulged. Such a counselor will not divulge your affairs if yot
retain him. (Distrust a broker or other adviser who does no
keep other clients' identities and affairs secret; he is likely to b
as openmouthed with yours.)

Sometimes a counselor will—with his client's permission—
show the names of one or two whose affairs he guides. If thes
investors will talk, they can help you to form a judgment of th
counselor's talents or lack of ability.

(3) At what kind of study is the adviser best? An adviser migh
guide clients on trends of the economy, the stock market, or th
choice of individual stocks and bonds to buy. One man is seldon
expert in all three fields, although most will offer guidance ir
all of them. Even sizable firms with large staffs do not ofter

shine in all areas; their heads, consciously or unconsciously, tend to feel that one field of expertise is overpoweringly important and hire employees who hold a similar view. The best staff members will be put into the effort the top men consider most productive for clients.

It becomes important for you to establish in what area you wish help and seek a service that concentrates on this discipline and has developed greatest skill at it. Economic and stock-market-trend projections are easiest to follow; judgments in these areas can be made from the public record. (Don't let anyone tell you that such areas aren't important or that the proper field for a counselor's endeavors is investment selection and not market direction. Anyone who suffered in the falling markets of the turn of the 1970 decade will testify that this is not so.)

(4) Is size a factor? Sometimes the small adviser with a one-man office gives closest individual attention and can shine in his field as compared with the committee approach of bigger firms. But don't let the jokes about committee approach influence you too much. Individual dispensers of professional wisdom are good when they are brilliant but worse than large staffs under other circumstances.

There are counselors and counseling firms that advertise widely. Others cloak themselves with the professional dignity assumed by physicians, dentists, lawyers, and architects; they will not advertise or countenance among their ranks any public display. That does not make them either better or worse as advisers for the average investor.

TIPS ON KEEPING COMMISSIONS LOW

Given the fact that certain advisers have built-in interest in commission building and that the activities of others will generate—sometimes to the investor's benefit—greater commission activity than the accepted practice of buying and holding stocks, it is well to know how commissions can be kept low:

(1) Avoid low-priced stocks. This seems heresy to a generation of investors trained to believe that better action comes in the low-priced group of stocks, which Wall Streeters derisively call cats and dogs.

Since commissions are set up by the 100-share round lot and not by the dollar amount bought and sold, simple arithmetic shows the extra amount a broker makes on low-priced equities at commission rates prevailing as this is written:

Take a $3,000 purchase. If you were to buy 1,000 shares of a $3 stock, you would pay, at commission rates obtaining in late 1971, $90 plus a $15 service charge, or $105. Percentage is 3.5% Assuming a buy and sell at the same figure, you would pay $210 or 7 percent.

If the $3,000 purchase consisted of 100 shares of a stock at $30 commissions would come to $34, plus a $15 service charge, or $49 Percentage would be 1.64, with 3.28 percent assessed on a round turn. The dollar saving would come to $76 to buy and another $76 to sell.

(2) Deal with one of the newer firms which eschew research and other services to give buy and sell representation at cut prices. The brochure of one house explained: "The firm's intention is to provide low commission rates related to the cost of each transaction. Accordingly, the following rules apply: (1) No margin accounts will be accepted; (2) No discretionary accounts will be accepted; and (3) Execution will occur only while the client is in personal or telephone contact with the firm or can be reached personally on the telephone. This firm generally does not hold securities for individual accounts. That is one reason it can offer reduced commissions."

Discounts from established commission rates offered by this firm ranged from 12 percent to 60 percent. Another firm offers service on an annual fee rather than per-trade basis. A third will handle odd-lot (less than 100-share) transactions at fees lower than charged by the established brokers.

These discount stores have no frills or fancy services, but prices frequently are lower. That matters.

(3) If buying mutual funds, use no-loads rather than load funds to save front-end commissions. Don't let a broker tell you that investors receive something extra in the way of service from the load funds. *He* makes commission on these.

Chapter 7

A SMALL INVESTOR
CAN MAKE IT BIG

A little investor can swing big weight by a technique unknown by most and feared by the few who do know what it can accomplish. The technique is leverage. Not the kind that Archimedes had in mind when he offered to move the world if someone would give him a fulcrum and a place to stand while he was performing, but the kind with which one dollar is able to do the work of two, three, four, five, or six.

Leverage comes about through the use of techniques and combinations of techniques explained below. These allow moderate funds to do the work of a great deal of capital. When the user of leverage is right, he can grow rich very swiftly, just as a plunger does when he lets a bet ride time after winning time at the tables in Las Vegas. If the plunger's luck or skill deserts him, however, he can suddenly bust, as can a plunger in the investment world of the new Wall Street, dominated in the seventies and eighties by giant institutions.

Therefore a warning: Don't plunge using heavy leverage, because a single bad investment, even a series that turn sour, can wreck your program and leave you bereft of the capital with which you started. Leverage works two ways: It is wonderful when you win; it can be disastrous when you lose.

The investor with moderate capital who wants to increase that capital should use leverage *only in controlled measure,* being aware of its dangers as well as its potential. He should achieve a degree that suits his financial situation and his personality, for the risk one investor can bear with sang froid reduces another to a state of sleeplessness. How much leverage is good and how much constitutes overuse is a matter each investor should decide for himself. The important thing is to make a decision and follow it. And remember that the danger of leverage increases in a market not growth-oriented.

Remember too that leverage *can* make you rich.

THE KINDS OF INVESTMENT LEVERAGE

Simple Margin Simple margin is borrowing on a purchase of stocks. The Federal Reserve Board sets how much margin, or downpayment, a broker must secure. This power was put into the Fed's hands after the disastrous experience of 1929–1930 showed that a 10 percent margin was a shifting sand on which to build a sound stock structure. The rate has varied in the period after World War II from 50 percent to 100 percent. The 50 percent figure meant that an investor who purchased stocks costing $5,000 had to put up a "margin" of $2,500. The 100 percent rule meant he had to come up with the whole bag. The Fed sets margin rates by what it feels the economic situation to be. Generally, lower rates are stimulative of stock market speculation; higher rates dampen it. The margin rate power was formerly more important than it now is in controlling or unloosing market frenzy. With individual investors no longer dominating the market, changes have less effect, since institutions rarely use margin credit.

Even at relatively high percentages, simple margin can greatly increase profits but also heighten risk of an investment. Say you have $2,500 with which you want to buy a stock costing $50 per share. On an outright for-cash purchase you could obtain 50 shares, commission costs being additional. At 80 percent margin —an historically high figure—you could buy 62 shares (actually

62¼, but half-shares aren't offered). Assume that the stock appreciated ten points to $60. If you were to sell out the 50 shares bought without margin, you would profit by $500, less commission. On 62 shares bought at 80 percent margin, the gain would be $620, again with commissions to be deducted. The difference is a sizable 24 percent.

With that amount added to starting capital, the possibility would be enhanced for still greater gain at 80 percent margin on the next transaction, assuming wise choice of stock and a good grasp of market direction, so that the investment proved profitable. As transactions succeeded, an investor could expect considerably increased results from the use of this simplest of all ways to make moderate capital do a sizable job. He could look for greater potential when margin requirements are set lower than our assumed 80 percent—as in practice, they generally are.

Options Options come in many varieties. One is called a *warrant*. Warrants give their holders the right to buy set numbers of common shares at a preset price. A typical warrant might specify the right to purchase one share of American Mugwump at ten. When the stock is selling below that figure, the warrant has only a nominal value, since no one would turn in the warrant to buy stock at ten when he could obtain all he wanted on the New York Stock Exchange at eight. Under such circumstances, the warrant might trade at one, giving it value only in the hope of an eventual rise in Mugwump common.

If the common gets above the exercise price—in this case ten —then fireworks begin. The warrant will rise a point for each point rise in the common and if the common gets hot, then the warrant might rise even faster, perhaps to a premium of three or four over the exercise price, since speculators begin to look at the rise in American Mugwump as a process which will continue.

A point rise from the level of one is greater than a point rise from the level of ten, without even counting in the probable premium to which the warrant would go in the event of a sustained Mugwump bull trend. Thus our investor with $2,500 capital might be able to buy 250 shares of common at ten or 2,500 warrants at one. If American Mugwump reached twelve, the investor with 250 shares would have increased his starting capital by $500. An investor who purchased the 1,000 warrants

with $2,500 capital, would have increased his capital by $5,000
Warrants obviously offer great leverage to the investor who
wants to build small capital quickly. They as obviously offer great
danger. A compromise way to handle the situation, somewhere
between the cautious purchase of 250 shares of common at ten
and the plunging buy of 2,500 warrants at one, might be to purchase 200 shares of common and 500 additional warrants. Another
compromise would be to place $2,250 of the starting $2,500
capital in bonds or blue chips and to use $250 to buy enough
warrants to give as much participation in the stock's rise as
$2,500 would buy if placed in common shares; in this case lever-
age would have brought about lessened risk.

There is a way to increase the already big leverage inherent in
warrants. They can be purchased on margin if they are listed on
a stock exchange. The American's lists contain many warrants.
This ploy would further increase the large investor's already vast
leverage in a purchase of American Mugwump warrants. With
$2,500 capital at 80 percent margin, his purchasing power would
come to 3,125 warrants and his gain in the event of a rise in the
common stock from ten to twelve would be $6,250.

Taking the conservative approach, a cautious investor might
have put $2,300 of his $2,500 into blue-chip stocks or discount
bonds, leaving $200 to be placed in warrants bought on margin.
He would have been able to purchase 250 warrants and still
participate as fully in the common stock advance as the investor
purchasing all common shares with $2,500 capital. He would
have preserved $2,300 of his seed money, exposing only 8 percent
to the risk of investment in shaky but promising American
Mugwump.

Warrants are often available for blue-chip as well as blue-sky
stocks. One example is American Telephone and Telegraph; another is the big daddy of closed-end investment trusts, Tricontinental Corp.

Most warrants have set dates on which they expire. It pays to
know these, since as the warrant approaches the expiration date
its value as a call upon the future of the common stock obviously
decreases. A few warrants are perpetual. Tricontinental's warrants are in this class.

Other option tools are called Puts and Calls. A Put gives its purchaser the right to tender stock at a predetermined price to the one who sold him the option. A Call gives him the right to buy stock at an agreed figure from the option seller, who is called a "writer." Puts and Calls can be purchased for varying periods of time, from thirty days to half a year. Most are written for ninety days.

A Securities and Exchange Commission study of Put and Call trading showed that more than half of these options were never exercised. The stock might fail to go up (in the case of a Call) or down (when the purchaser holds a Put) sufficiently for an investor to show a profit during the life of the option. There are other cases in which the stock moves as expected but not enough to cover the cost of the Put or Call. In such a situation the option holder will exercise his Put or Call in order to lessen the loss.

A problem for investors is the high cost and short life of a Put or Call option. In a typical case, the option might be for ninety days and the cost from 12½ to 15 percent of the price of the stock. Taking a $40 stock as example, the buyer would pay about $550 for a Call on 100 shares. Unless the stock rose above 45½, he would lose money. Three months is a short period in which to expect spectacular stock price movement and in many cases the investor loses even though his homework was carefully done. And even if the price of the stock eventually goes as projected but stays in the doldrums only 91 days, the investor is behind.

Some investors use Puts and Calls for hedging, as when a Put is purchased to protect a paper profit. In such an event it's well to remember that as soon as the Put has been purchased, the paper profit has been reduced by the option cost. Danger to the gain will recommence the day the Put expires. (Investors "hedge" with options when they want to play both ends of the market. *Example:* An investor bought Stock A at 40, watched it climb to 60, and is now afraid that it may decline. But he's also afraid it will go up and he will miss out on additional profits. He might buy a Put, probably for $500. If the stock went down, he could offer his own stock, thus "losing" the cost of the option but saving the rest of the profit. If the stock went up, he would be out the cost of the Put, but still aboard a rising stock.)

A sounder way to utilize these options is to *sell* Puts in order to *buy* stocks. Through your local New York Stock Exchange member brokerage house, you can arrange to become a writer of options. Writing Puts as a means of buying stocks—but only those you intend to purchase in any case—can reduce the stock cost by the amount received from the purchaser for the option

The Put and Call dealer firm of Filer, Schmidt and Co., Inc. explained this in a brochure:

> There are two ways of buying stocks. One is the conventional method that most people use of merely putting in an order to buy stocks at a price or "at the market." On the other hand, there are numerous investors who acquire stocks by selling or giving an OPTION to possibly buy stocks at a price, in a given time, and for which OPTION, they receive a premium of so many dollars For instance, with U.S. Steel selling at 67, a man willing to buy Steel at or under 67, would sell someone the OPTION of delivering Steel to him at 67 any time in ninety days, for a cash premium of $325.00. The dollars thus received make an interesting percentage return on the amount of money involved. These OPTION contracts are known as PUT contracts. They are endorsed or guaranteed by member firms of the New York Stock Exchange and are transferable.
>
> To make the operation simple to understand, it might be interesting to lay out in table form, the acquisition of stocks, by two investors, in the two different ways already mentioned.
>
> Mr. A puts in orders to buy and does buy,

100 shares	U.S. Steel.............	at 67	$ 6,700.00
100 shares	General Motors........	at 47	4,700.00
100 shares	Montgomery Ward.....	at 42	4,200.00
100 shares	Republic Steel.........	at 55	5,500.00
100 shares	Chrysler..............	at 70	7,000.00
100 shares	Anaconda.............	at 83	8,300.00
100 shares	Jones & Laughlin.......	at 60	6,000.00
100 shares	Pepsi-Cola............	at 24	2,400.00
100 shares	Southern Railway......	at 42	4,200.00
100 shares	N.Y. Central.........	at 37	3,700.00

$52,700.00

Mr. B., who understands the selling of OPTIONS, would also like to buy the same list of stocks, but goes about it in a different way. He sells OPTION contracts . . . whereby, for a cash consideration paid to him, someone may deliver to Mr. B, at a fixed price, and in a specified time, stock which Mr. B would be willing to buy. . . . The amount of premium which Mr. B can receive varies according to the stock, its possible fluctuations, and the duration of the OPTION contract.

By way of comparison it might be interesting to set in chart form, the transactions made by Mr. B in selling these PUT OPTIONS in a desire to acquire the same stocks as those bought by Mr. A.

Sold Put Contract on 100 shares			*Prem. rec'd by Mr. B*
U.S. Steel	at 67	expires in 90 days	$ 325.00
General Motors	at 47	expires in 90 days	300.00
Montgomery Ward	at 42	expires in 90 days	275.00
Republic Steel	at 55	expires in 90 days	300.00
Chrysler	at 70	expires in 90 days	400.00
Anaconda	at 83	expires in 90 days	475.00
Jones & Laughlin	at 60	expires in 90 days	325.00
Pepsi-Cola	at 24	expires in 90 days	175.00
Southern Railway	at 42	expires in 90 days	225.00
N.Y. Central	at 37	expires in 90 days	200.00
			$3,000.00

The difference between the operations of Mr. A and Mr. B is this: Mr. A has bought $52,700.00 worth of stock which may go up or may go down. Mr. B has contracted to buy the same $52,700.00 worth of stocks but he has been paid $3,000.00 for the contract. At the end of the 90 day contract period one of two things will happen. Mr. B will be obliged to buy the above list of stocks for which he will have to pay $52,700.00 but his cost will be reduced by the $3,000.00 in premiums which he has received. Mr. A's cost is not reduced and still remains at $52,700.00. Mr. B has bought the same stock as Mr. A at a net cost of $49,700.00. The other possibility in connection with the sale of these PUT contracts is that they might not be exercised and Mr. B will not be called upon to buy the stocks. In that event, Mr. B's cash of $52,700.00 which was set aside for the purchase of these stocks will have earned him $3,000.00 in ninety days or at the annual rate of over 22%.

Mouth-watering, isn't it? Before you get too carried away, remember that high risks are involved in the use of Puts and Calls and that if things don't do as expected *within the time limit of the options,* every dollar put into these risk-potential investments can go up in smoke.

Convertibles   Convertible preferreds and bonds are another means for securing added leverage and making an investment dollar do the work of more than the value printed on its face.

Convertibles can usually be bought on smaller margin than the common stock. When the stock goes up, a convertible which is tied to it will generally advance also. There is a safety kicker in addition to leverage when an investor buys convertibles because these have an accepted investment value of their own—based upon the yield at which they sell and their ratings as straight income instruments—and will not often decline as much as the common in a bear trend.

Profit Leverage   Leverage is inherent in the capital structures of some corporations. *Example:* A company with heavy debt has to struggle to bring in enough to pay out the creditors and there is seldom much left around for stockholders to divide among themselves in the form of dividends. Earnings are typically low. But not all the time. Assume that our company suddenly emerges into the clear daylight of a new fad in which its product is not only in demand but also in short supply. When an event like that impends, strong leverage can go to work. After the heavy debt charges have been passed, the big new volume and consequently increased gross profits are easily brought down to net and the earnings can increase much faster than the percentage of sales gain.

The same kind of profit leverage (but only past a breakeven point) occurs in companies with old equipment and inefficient processes that make them compete poorly in ordinary times. If extraordinary times come along, the firm grows suddenly profitable. Leverage has been at work.

Dual Funds   Dual funds offer leverage on their capital shares because, with all the gains working for only one group of stockholders, a rising market or a market favorable to the type of company represented in the dual fund's portfolio can bring added rise in net-asset valuation applicable to the capital shares.

LEVERAGE IN A BEAR MARKET

In a market whose major trend is down and in which prices erode, slide, and slip day after day, leverage is a way to early financial death unless you follow these courses:

(1) Stay away from leverage on the long side. When you are "long," that means that you have bought and own the securities.

(2) Employ margin leverage for selling short securities you don't have, in expectation of a decline. If and when the decline becomes an actuality, you will be able to buy them at less than you received when you sold. Short selling is the reverse of the classic advice to an investor to buy low and sell dear. In short selling, he sells dear and then hopes to buy low. If the stock does not go down, he loses money. The man who buys at what he believes to be a low figure, only to see the price go lower instead of running to the dear level, also loses money.

It is more difficult to get off a short than it was in the frantic decade of the sixties. There are two causes. The first is the Securities and Exchange Commission's uptick rule. Under this rule, Big Bear can't sell a stock short except at a tick higher than the previous sale. Assume that American Mugwump stock traded at 39⅞. Unless that price was an uptick from the previous trade, in which case Big Bear could go short at 39⅞, he would have to wait until he could get off the short at least one-eighth point (12½ cents) per share higher than the preceding sale. In a sliding bear market, it is not always easy to find uptick spots at prices where bears want to short; the opportunity of selling, which seems so glittering at 39⅞, has less glitter if the stock should drop to 35 before trading at an uptick. When placing a short-sale order it is wise to give the broker a limit below which the short is not to be made.

A more serious obstacle to short selling in the present era is the difficulty of obtaining borrowed stock. When Big Bear sells short 100 American Mugwump common, he expects to receive stock he purchased. To accomplish this, Big Bear's broker borrows stock which has been pledged by a margin customer. Standard margin agreements give him this power.

There was plenty of stock around to be lent in the happy, halcyon days of the middle and late sixties, when there were 30 million small investors and individual margin accounts were loaded with stocks. Came bear days and the increased institutional dominance of trading. Institutions' stocks are rarely margined but bought for cash, locked up, and unavailable for lending. Investors found it hard to borrow. There is danger in today's market that stock lent to you may be wanted when its owner decides to sell and that no stock will be available to replace it. Then the broker will have to purchase in the open market to cover.

Short-sellers bear a cost not borne by people who buy stocks, whether with leverage or not. The owner of a stock receives dividends declared by the company's board of directors. The short-seller of the same stock *pays* a dividend when it comes due. This happens because two people "own" the stock he is short—the broker's margin customer from whom stock was borrowed to deliver on his short sale, and the buyer who purchased when he went short. Since the company pays only one dividend on the same stock and two stockowners look for the payout, money to satisfy one comes from the short-seller.

Short-selling is a workable way to seek profits in a bear market trend provided the stock is widely held and the broker believes (although he won't often promise) that you won't be called for borrowed stock. Shorting is one workable way to employ leverage during a downtrend.

(3) Or you can purchase puts, the limited-term options described in this chapter. A put is subject to all the dangers mentioned earlier. Things being equal, I advise short-selling as the better alternative.

(4) Capital shares of dual funds, good leverage plays during a market uptrend, offer interesting potential as a downside play during bear trends.

(5) Warrants should be avoided on a downtrend or sold short. When to employ leverage methods applicable to a bull market and when to switch to the use of those methods suitable for a downtrend will be covered in detail in a future chapter on determining the directions of bull and bear tides.

Chapter 8

OPPORTUNITY OUTSIDE
THE U.S.A.

Say "offshore" and most people think of rigs that dot the Gulf of Mexico and California's Pacific coast, and sometimes burn or spill oil to the detriment of fish, men, and onshore property owners. To investors, "offshore" offers little spill but much opportunity.

The United States once enjoyed the fastest growth in the world. In the late sixties, other nations began to outstrip American manufacturing and selling of goods. The economies of Japan, Germany, and others grew faster and waxed fatter. Goods from offshore flooded American stores. American corporations often moved to lands where taxes were lower and labor less costly. The result was—and is—development of tremendous investing opportunity. It exists today and should continue unless there is war or other cataclysm.

WHY INVEST OVERSEAS?

Reasons for investing overseas can be found in figures and word pictures like these:

Things are booming Down Under. Most people have undoubtedly read reports of the spectacular antics of mining shares listed on Australian exchanges; those more closely in touch with the country will have realized that the Australian economy is currently undergoing a dramatic transformation based primarily on its burgeoning mineral industry. Vast mineral deposits have now been discovered in many parts of the continent and, as a result of developments over the past decade, Australia has won impressive new status as one of the world's leading mining nations with a supply potential perhaps as great as, if not greater than, that of Canada.

Taking a close second place to iron ore in the mining picture has been the bauxite-aluminum industry. Developments since the discovery of bauxite deposits at Weipa in Northern Queensland in 1955 have turned Australia into a major world source, and have given rise to a whole new domestic aluminum industry. Thus far, over $600 millions have been invested in the industry but existing plans should lift this figure to $1 billion early in the 1970's, after which time still further expansion is anticipated.

Nickel is one of the newest arrivals on the Australian mining scene but, since the first strike at Kambalda, W.A., in February 1966 a great many things have happened. . . . companies, including the large Canadian producers, are now engaged in intensive exploration programs. Geologists have already proved a great nickel belt in the vicinity of Kalgoorlie (once famed as a gold mining centre) with characteristics similar to those in the rich mineral-bearing zone of the Canadian Shield.

In 1965 Australia's first really large deposits of oil and natural gas were found beneath the turbulent waters of Bass Strait off the south-east coast of Victoria. Since then production has grown rapidly, although not enough to meet total domestic needs which are expected to increase by 75% in the next decade. The search for new deposits continues. (From: "Australia . . . Minerals Galore," April, 1970, *Monthly Review*, Bank of Nova Scotia, Toronto, Canada.)

Founded in the mid-seventeenth century as a halfway house of the seas to supply ships on the spice route to the East, South Africa has moved on to become an indispensable link in modern trade across the oceans and to join the top seventeen trading nations of the world.

Today South Africa delivers not only ships' supplies, but also uranium, isotopes, vaccines, textiles, heavy machinery . . .

South Africa produces and consumes more steel and electricity than the rest of the continent put together. Her industries turn out a wide range of products from automotive parts and explosives to synthetic rubber and vanadium pentoxide. One of the world's largest oil-from-coal plants is located here. The Republic has attained indisputable industrial leadership in Africa.

With a large share of all foreign investment in Africa, the Republic provides the most comprehensive transport system, nearly half of the continent's telephones and vehicles, and know-how which is available to all countries on the continent of Africa which have the desire to benefit from it. (From: "South Africa on the Move," an advertisement in the *Wall Street Journal.*)

Japanese trading companies are the Oriental version of multinational corporations. A typical Japanese trading company sells the business machines of Sperry Rand's Italian, Dutch and French affiliates to Japan; UMS soybeans to Taiwan and Germany; California rice to Okinawa. It sells Ford trucks to Indonesia and finds markets for Indonesian agricultural products to provide means for repayment. It exports American soybeans to the Philippines, and after local processing sells the by-products to other Far Eastern countries. Japanese trading firms have a wide information-gathering network which enables them to seize every opportunity to buy, stock, hedge, transfer and sell. While Japan's dependence on exports is considerably lower (at 10 percent of GNP) than most industrialized European nations (which range from 15 to 30 percent), Japanese trading companies have become more and more vigorously engaged in channeling goods from one part of the world to another. (From: "The Japanese Economy Goes International," an advertisement in the *Wall Street Journal*.)

The growth of Mexico's gross national product in 1969 was 6.4% at constant prices, a higher rate than that of population growth (3.4%). At current prices, Mexico's GNP reached the record figure of U.S. $29,000m. Per capita output in 1969 was U.S. $613.

Investment maintained a high rate of growth, and accounted for approximately 21% of GNP with domestic savings financing more than 90%.

Industrial activity was the most dynamic element in the economy, and the supply of services responded to increases in demand. The industrial sector represents 28% of GNP in comparison with 24% in 1960. The relative importance of services within the economy has remained stable during the decade. (From: *Mexico 1970*, a government brochure.)

Europe also is an offshore avenue of investment. Its people have repeatedly been counted out, from the time when Germany was ravaged by the Thirty Years War to the encompassing destruction in World War II. "The direction in which to look for tomorrow's land of prosperity is southward," thundered some American observers after World War II had ground to a halt. "Latin America is the land of the future. Europe is done for."

They were as wrong as were the men who wrote off Germany after the Thirty Years War and those who saw France as an unimportant, poor power after Prussian armies had beaten her in 1870. Europe came back. It is a land of energetic people, technological discovery, and restless competitiveness.

Emerging nations' statistics dazzle the eye and make an investor forget the solid opportunities in a mature area such as Europe. It is not the purpose of this book to discuss the social desirability of investment in emerging nations. From the *business* viewpoint of solidity combined with relative safety of capital and relative excellence of return, the nations of Europe deserve consideration. Consider these figures (source, *Rates of Change in Economic Data for Ten Industrial Countries* prepared by the Federal Reserve Bank of St. Louis):

From March, 1966 to February, 1971, Belgium's industrial production enjoyed a 5.3 *average compounded* rate of growth *per year*. France enjoyed a rate of 5.6 percent during the period. The figure for Germany was 6.7 percent, for Italy 4.0 percent, for the Netherlands 9.1 percent, for Switzerland 5.6 percent, for the United Kingdom 2.1 percent. The figure for the United States during this time was 1.1 percent, and for Canada 3.7 percent average compounded rate of industrial production growth per year.

THERE ARE DRAWBACKS, TOO

Even in advanced lands, anti-American feeling enters with the American capital which is at first desired, then later resented. One Canadian authority called it a "love-hate" relationship. "On the one hand," he said, "we have from the beginning welcomed foreign capital. On the other hand, there have been over the years waves of resentment about the degree of dependence upon foreigners."

Given such a love-hate relationship, stocks of American companies having foreign commitments are subject to occasional waves of selling brought on by politicians' expounding of the hate part of the relationship.

Economic nationalism is not the only drawback to investment off U.S. shores. Another difficulty is the paucity of information available to investors. There are few facts to be had and figures are frequently unbelievable, although companies with stocks traded in the United States and Canada who must care about the attitudes of North American investigators tend to do less hiding of assets and profits. Sometimes big investors find that it pays to hire investment advice in the countries where they are putting money, in the hope that these pros will be in touch with men who run the companies and thus be able to make evaluations that investors across the water cannot do competently. As often as not, the hopes prove vain.

Another drawback is the frequent non-liquidity of offshore stocks. It would be possible to buy and sell blocks of thousands of shares of leading North American companies, but often investors find that foreign—particularly European—stocks must be broken into bits and fed out to the market a little at a time even where the blocks are small.

According to the comment of one Frankfort-headquartered U.S. broker, Europeans tend to invest in American stocks not because they think more highly of prospects but because they can be readily bought and sold.

HOW TO GET AROUND THE DIFFICULTIES

Mutual Funds and Investment Trusts   One way to avoid difficulties is through purchase of offshore mutual funds and investment trusts, closed or open-end. If you like the prospects for South Africa, to take one example, American-South African Investment is a closed-end listed on the New York Stock Exchange. Its package of Cape of Good Hope securities is gold-oriented. If you're sold on the Common Market and other fast-moving areas of the world (see statistics above on growth of industrial production) consider Eurofund International. Japan Fund offers a group of Far Eastern securities and participation in the dynamics of that area of the world. There are many other geographical funds which give portfolio packages of securities in specific areas of the world. They have the advantage of local staffs with local insights into problems and opportunities that analysts headquartered in New York or other financial centers of North America might find hard to match. Additionally, they offer the mutual fund advantage of diversification that an individual investor could not easily achieve on his own.

American Depositary Receipts   Difficulties may also be avoided by means of American Depositary Receipts. A bank, usually in New York, holds foreign securities. Against these it issues "ADR's" which are traded in North American markets in the same way stocks themselves can be bought and sold. There is no problem with collection of dividends from overseas—the bank takes these in and disburses them to ADR holders—or any of the frustrating, time-consuming routine of registration which can be much more complicated in other places than in the United States and Canada.

ADR trading has been active in New York since the 1920's. It has accelerated in recent years as the economies of many lands have merged into one interacting global economy. American Depositary Receipts are beginning to be traded on U.S. exchanges, making them as easy to own and dispose of as securities of American or Canadian companies.

Multinational Corporations Multinational corporations are a development of recent years. Many are big U.S.-based companies which have expanded into Europe, Canada, and other parts of the world to secure local capital, to take advantage of lower labor costs elsewhere, and always to market more effectively. Now the flow of multinational operations is coming to us across the Atlantic and Pacific. German, English, French, Italian, Japanese, and other companies are finding that the best way to tap North American markets is from a North American location. Royal Dutch-Shell and Unilever have done this for years.

The proliferation of multinational corporations offers investors a play in other countries without the sometimes cumbersome mechanics of buying and holding stocks from those areas. It has disadvantages, too. The multinational company has to live with laws, peculiarities, and ways of a great diversity of nations. Yet most times it remains a company of its country of origin, and developments there have a greater effect upon its fortunes than occurrences elsewhere.

Table 6, a rundown of typical multinationals, shows comparative sales from the United States and from foreign operations during 1970.

Foreign Bank Deposits Foreign bank deposits grew in popularity as the United States dollar declined in domestic purchasing power and in the regard of foreign bankers during the 1969–1971 period. Just as there are times when a reserve held in cash in a bank can be the soundest way to employ money temporarily in the United States (short-term investments will receive greater attention in the next chapter), occasions arise when to preserve wealth or await opportunity, a foreign bank account is highly useful. Swiss accounts are popular. All these are not the

TABLE 6. COMPARATIVE SALES OF TYPICAL
MULTINATIONALS

Company	Net sales, in millions	Foreign sales, in millions	Operations
E. I. du Pont	$ 3,618	$ 634	North American, Europe
Minnesota Mining	1,687	605	Europe, Canada, Australia
General Motors	18,751	3,563	Worldwide
Ford	14,980	3,900	Britain, Germany, Australia
Standard Oil (N.J.)	16,554	8,277	Worldwide
General Foods	2,282	479	U.S., Canada

super-secret numbered variety. Nor are they used exclusively by mysterious Mafia figures to hide loot from tax collectors and district attorneys. They are highly respectable.

There was a time in the 1969–1971 period when German marks rose in value vis-à-vis U.S. dollars. An investor possessing a foreign bank account *which held his deposit in marks rather than dollars* would have profited quickly. So would an investor using an overseas account as a way of holding Swiss francs or other currencies which, after devaluation of the U.S. dollar, rose in relation to our battered currency of the time. To hold funds in foreign currencies, you instruct your Swiss or other foreign banker to credit the currency—marks, pounds, francs, yen, lira— of your choice, converting the dollars you send into that money.

U.S. laws change and so do those of other countries. It is well to acquaint yourself with legal hedges and demands before opening an account in foreign currency. Talk also to your local banker and to the consulate of the country chosen to be a temporary investment capital haven. There are dangers as well as opportunities, of course. Profits come to those knowledgeable about changes in currency exchange rates.

Chapter 9

SOMETIMES THE
SHORT TERM IS BEST

A great controversy arose in one southern state. An alert (and vote-minded) politician had discovered that hundreds of millions of dollars of state deposit money had been parceled out to banks, often on the basis of favor, and that the banks were paying no interest on these funds which swelled their deposit figures.

"Disgraceful!" he thundered. "That money might bring in 6 percent—and it could produce even more. On an average of about 250 million dollars that state banks are holding in interest-free deposits, the state is losing $15 million a year. Think what that could mean in relief from some of our high taxes! Think what it would produce in the way of a needed raise for teachers or for our underpaid policemen and struggling civil service workers! Short-term deposits should bring in money for the state just as they would for a private investor."

On the basis of such oratorical fireworks and a favorable press that adopted his slogan of "Let's *invest* the state's money," he was shortly elected to the legislature. Periodically, he spoke for the cause. The periods lengthened out. Not too long after achieving office, he started a small bank of his own into which state deposits poured—interest free. No more was heard of the merits of short-term investing of monies not needed for normal operation.

His cause remained a sound one, although it was allowed to die—and although he had erred badly in saying that private investors regularly put their short-term funds to work producing income. Few do. Many would be better off if they did. In the troubled, changeable, new world of investing ahead, occasions arise when the prudent course is to withdraw money from the market and from other media and hold it in reserve for a time. Examples are easy to find: In 1962, 1966, 1969–1970, and the latter half of 1971 when cash appreciated vis-à-vis stocks and was therefore a prime holding (more on choosing such times in Chapter 12). During such periods of holding all or partial commitment to cash reserve, the cash should earn something.

There are other occasions for short-term cash investment. You have sold a house and plan to buy another. After settling the old mortgage, you have $10,000 in cash which you feel you cannot put into stocks or other long-term investments because you expect to need the money shortly, in part as downpayment on your new home and in part as payment for remodeling, changes and improvements you plan to make. Don't put it into an ordinary bank checking account at no interest when it can bring in a hefty yield *even when invested for as little as thirty days.* (A parenthetical word: Ordinary bank savings accounts are not, under generally prevailing conditions, ideal for holding short-term money. The reason is that you must leave funds in a savings account until expiration of a quarter—March 31, June 30, September 30, December 31—in order to draw interest on them. There are some exceptions; if your bank pays interest to date of withdrawal, then disregard this caveat.)

"For those few available pennies?" a reader might ask.

The answer is that pennies soon mount to dollars and that in a total strategy of striving for gains during the new days ahead, each kind of gain has a place in the plan—not least, the achievement of profit on short-term investment of money available during limited periods or held for a need sure to arise at an early date.

On a November morning in 1971, the following yields (about

average for those of the present era) were available on short-term instruments: Commercial paper of thirty to ninety days— 6 to 7½ percent. Treasury Bills of six months—5.2 percent; Bills of three months—4.8 percent (Bills have been as high as 8 percent in recent times). Banker's acceptances of one to 180 days—6¾ percent.

These are juicy yields, and they are liquid. Short-term investments can be tailored to the length of time an investor expects to have the surplus cash available. Moreover, most of these investment instruments are sufficiently salable that a market may be had for them if it is necessary to convert back to cash before the time you have targeted.

Treasury Bills are short-term debt instruments of the United States. They are issued in maturities of three months to one year. Banker's acceptances are debt instruments used to finance export, import, and storage and movement of goods. They are issued and become "accepted" when a bank guarantees their payment at maturity. Commercial paper is issued by corporations to finance month-to-month needs; much of it is issued by financing firms, but a great deal comes from other types of business as well. The credit of commercial paper is as good as that of the corporation issuing it. Short-term tax-exempts are paper somewhat like Treasury Bills but with the feature of having income exempt from federal taxation as is the interest on longer-term municipal bonds.

Other short-term paper is issued by semigovernmental bodies, such as the Federal National Mortgage Association. Banks frequently tailor CD's—Certificates of Deposit—for terms as short as one month.

Treasury Bills give you probably the highest quality short-term debt instrument you can buy. They are direct Treasury obligations. Bills are issued only in $10,000 denominations, and can be bought in any multiple of that number. Purchasing Bills is done this way:

You instruct your broker or your bank to buy X-thousand dollars of Bills next week, specifying the maturity (three months to a year) you wish. The Treasury sells these each week. You will get a confirmation saying you bought your investment at a stated percentage. This means that you pay less than $10,000 for a $10,000 Bill—how much less depending upon the maturity and upon the interest rate at which the auction closed—and then, at maturity, the Bills are redeemed for full face value. The difference between these two prices is not a capital gain. It is considered interest for tax purposes. (This method of buying below face value, with redemption at par, holds for most investment media for short-term surplus cash.)

When the Bills mature you will get a check, if you want it, from the bank or broker through whom you purchased them. But first, the banker or broker will telephone you to advise you on the coming maturity of your Bills and ask: "Shall I roll them over?" Rolling over means purchase with the proceeds of the new issue coming on sale the same day your current Bills mature. If you want the proceeds for operational needs, just say "No." If the cash stays in surplus, you can order a rollover for the new issue unless at the time better yields are available elsewhere.

Regarding Bills, people ask these questions:

Q. *Suppose we roll them over, then two weeks afterward the funds are required. Are we locked in until maturity?*

A. No. The Treasury won't cash you up, but a regular market for Bills exists and they can be sold as readily as stocks or bonds. You will probably be able to realize your accrued interest at time of sale, although this is not certain, since the sale price will depend upon money-market conditions at the moment.

Q. *What advantage, if any, have banker's acceptances over Treasury Bills?*

A. The name of this particular game is money, and score is kept by how much of it you can make your surplus capital bring in. Banker's acceptances offer more (although not a great deal more) money than you could realize by investing temporarily extra investment capital in Treasury Bills.

Q. *By how much?*

A. On December 15, 1971, three-month Treasury Bills were worth 4.8 percent. Banker's acceptances brought 6.3 percent.

Q. *Wouldn't we be taking a bigger risk in acceptances than in Bills?*

A. Yes—but only infinitesimally. The credit of the nation's biggest banks is very high, and you run a risk of only one to three months.

*Q. I can buy Bills with $10,000 extra cash. Can I get into the
acceptances market with such an ante?*

A. Not usually. If your bank or broker can obtain $25,000 in
acceptances for you, he will have done very well. Most often it
is a market for well-heeled investing corporations. The ante usually begins in six figures. If you have surplus cash that high, however, the banker's acceptance market might be a lucrative one.

For commercial paper you usually (not always—see below)
need a bigger stake, too, than in the Treasury Bill game. Commercial paper is unsecured, short-term debt of corporations—
some the biggest and best on the list. They can raise funds easily
in this way and are often willing to pay slightly higher rates than
on regular bank loans. Commercial paper affords them flexibility;
the debt structure can be quickly expanded or shrunk with commercial paper. So you, as investor of sometimes temporarily available funds, benefit with good yields of the kind outlined above.

But unlike the situation in banker's acceptances, there is greater
access to the market for the smaller investor. Sometimes banks
will band many clients together into a pool, charging a minimal
fee, and buy blocks of acceptances to give small- to medium-sized
investors and companies a chance at the juicy yields that commercial paper offers.

If you do sit in this game, either directly or through an inter-
mediary bank or brokerage firm, you can find yields in the 7 to 8
percent area. An old rule of thumb on how long it takes money
to double itself at compound interest calls for dividing the interest rate into the number 72. Doing such a computation with 8
percent yields shows a doubling in nine years.

You are not likely to tie up surplus funds that long and it isn't
likely that such whopping big yields will be available over an
extended period of time. But it is mind-expanding to realize that
a yield obtainable now on short-term surplus investable funds is
large enough to double capital in less than nine years.

Tax-exempt short-term paper is the so-called municipal bonds
—the bonds of cities, states, counties, special authorities, school
districts, and the like. Their interest is exempt from federal income taxation and often from taxation in the state of issue as
well. These bonds were discussed earlier.

Another source of short-term tax-exempt paper is the Department of Housing and Urban Development, which sells notes on behalf of local housing agencies. Bidders are usually big banks. You may be able to obtain a participation through your local bank or brokerage house. But they won't usually want to let you into this game without an opening stack of chips totaling $100,000 or more.

Both this short-term paper and those of semigovernmental agencies are instruments of indebtedness, both carry high interest rates today, and both groups are issued by governmental bodies. Their differences are that they are issued by different sorts of governmental bodies—tax-exempt paper by states, cities, and the like and semigovernmentals by federal agencies such as the Federal National Mortgage Association. They differ additionally in that FNMA paper and paper of other semigovernmental bodies are not exempt from federal income taxation.

Then why buy FNMA's? That would depend upon your tax problems. In certain circumstances, the tax exemption matters. In others, the higher yield that FNMA's and semigovernmentals pay is the prevailing factor in a decision for short-term investment.

The yield on semigovernmentals will depend upon conditions of the time, of course. Semigovernmental agency bonds usually offer from one to two percent higher yields than are obtainable on direct Treasury obligations. This spread tends to shrink as you get to the short-term group, however, and the differential for short-term paper might be from one-half to one percent.

Remember that quoted yields are generally "yield to maturity," which was discussed in Chapter 5.

Bank Certificates of Deposit have good and bad points. The Federal Reserve System has placed top limits on what they will pay in interest to get money—through Certificates of Deposit or otherwise—and for many kinds of investors, this has put CD's out of the competitive running.

At times when Treasury Bill yields are historically high, the yields on Certificates of Deposit are generally lower. But when Bill yields drop, they generally go down faster than CD yields. For a time at least, then, there are situations when the favorable spread is on Certificates.

Whether they pay more or less than the yield for Treasury

Bills, CD's have certain important advantages as interest-paying havens for temporary capital. They can be tailored to any maturity you want—this depends upon the terms you can work with your local bank—from thirty days upward. And they are available in odd amounts, unlike Treasury Bills, which must be purchased in multiples of $10,000, or acceptances and commercial paper which come in even higher amounts. If you have $1,868 which you wish to put to work for the next month, chances are that you can find a bank willing to write a CD in this amount and for that maturity.

But be aware of one thing: The CD is not as liquid as the Treasury Bill or as any other piece of marketable debt paper. If you need that $1,868 after expiration of two weeks, the banker is likely to shake his head. "Sorry," he'll say, "we can't do it. But I will write a loan for the amount you want, using the Certificate of Deposit as security." He will charge about two percent higher interest than he pays you. Thus you can wipe out any interest advantage you expected and can even, depending upon the length of time your borrowing goes on, end up paying interest for the use of your own money.

Certificates of Deposit are flexible as to amounts and maturities but not as to marketability during the time they run. (Bigger CD's can be marketed at need, but usually only at severe discounts because they are, like an out-of-fashion dress in a retail store's inventory, distress merchandise and the purchaser is aware of that fact.)

Bonds can also be used for short-term purposes. You choose bonds having a maturity approximately as long as the time you are willing to have the short-term capital tied up. For example: you have $5,000 which you want to have liquid in three months. You take out the morning paper, turn to the financial section, and find there a table of semigovernment agency bonds such as Fannie Mae. There you see a longer-term bond which expires in the time you wish. The price on it might be 99, and there would be some interest remaining after you paid accrued interest to the investor from whom you bought. The yield is right, the maturity is right. You incur a commission charge, which might be slightly higher than you would pay to buy a Treasury Bill of the same maturity.

On the day this is written—one of prevailing yields typical of the period we are discussing—the following were obtainable from bonds which, although of longer-term, had close-in maturities:

A Treasury Bond maturing in three months—5 percent

A Federal Land Bank bond maturing in three months—5.1 percent

A FNMA debenture maturing in one month—3.7 percent

A FNMA maturing in three months—4.8 percent

A Eurodollar is an American dollar held in a European bank. Lent on a short-term basis, Eurodollars frequently bring in higher interest payments than those conventionally available. Say you had a deposit of $1 million in a bank having a branch located in London. If you instructed this bank to put your money into its London branch, your dollars would immediately become Eurodollars. In the March, 1968, issue of its *Monthly Review,* the Federal Reserve Bank of San Francisco estimated the volume of Eurodollars at $200 million. The amount has grown vastly since then.

In November, 1971, a New York Stock Exchange member firm which is active in underwritings began to market commercial paper denominated in Eurodollars. "Euro-commercial paper"— that's what they call it—is available under the names of many prestigious United States corporations.

There are many ways for idle money to bring you capital gains instead of "mere" income. But such funds as we have discussed here are available for a short time only, since they are needed in the near future. Seeking capital gains involves more risk. Such money unduly risked brings on possible loss of these funds.

If you have a craving for high risk, however, and a sum which can be reasonably risked, try the Puts and Calls market. We discussed them earlier. An example: You become convinced that a stock is going up from its present price of $40. A Call option would entitle you to buy, or call, for the stock at a prearranged price (usually market price at the time the Call is purchased) for anywhere from thirty days to six months. Say you buy a 90-day Call for $400 on 100 shares of the $40 stock. If it goes to 50, you have made $600, less the cost of commissions to exercise the Call, buy the stock at $4,000, then re-sell it at $5,000 ($1,000 raw gain less $400 cost of the Call). It is a nice, neat 150 percent gain in three months, a profit that would annualize at 600 percent. But if the price didn't go up—or worse, if it waited out your three-month period, then put on an appreciation spurt—you would be out the whole amount invested in the Call.

I'm not recommending that anyone do this. It is a way to employ part of idle capital in active speculation *if* you feel that temporary speculation is a thing you want to do with temporarily sidelined funds.

Chapter 10

PLANNING FOR

AFFLUENT RETIREMENT

Y ou can't count on automati-
cally affluent retirement. It takes a lot of planning. A pension
isn't enough. Neither—if you want affluent living after retirement
—is social security. Both together might do the job, but in view
of dangers to which pension funds are exposed, they might not.

THE DANGER TO THE PENSION

Pensions to which employees and/or companies contribute are
subject to the obvious danger of inflation. The constant dwindling
in purchasing power of our dollars, sometimes slowed and occasionally stifled to the seeming stop point, only to break out into
raging fire shortly afterward, is a phenomenon of post-World
War II life everywhere, which more than any other fact has
wrecked the hopes of affluent retirement for millions. It isn't the
only peril. Congressional hearings have revealed a danger which
threatens the receipt of *any* retirement benefit for millions of
Americans.

Senator Jacob Javits (New York) pointed out in a hearing before the Labor Subcommittee Pension Study of the Joint Eco-

nomic Committee of the Congress of the United States, on April 5, 1971:

> . . . it is a rare thing to find a major American Institution —private pension plans—built upon human disappointment—a shocking thing, and something which should move us all to act with determination to make that institution deliver upon its promises.
>
> . . . Even in an "earlier vesting" sample, in which 16 percent of those who left were protected from forfeitures, there were included in the balance 36,901 employees who worked more than 10 years and got nothing—not a large percentage of the whole, but human beings nevertheless, moving into their older years without the protection they should have had.
>
> No doubt as this study proceeds further the statistics will be refined and amplified. But even as this first flash of daylight begins to reach into the long-hidden statistical truth of the private pension plan industry, it ought to be obvious that something is wrong, and that it needs to be set right.
>
> . . . *As things now stand, only a relative handful of the estimated tens of millions of American workers under private pension plans will ever get anything from the plans on which they now stake their futures.* [Italics supplied.]

Even pension plans of bigger companies, in which employees have vesting, sometimes prove illusory to those who depend upon them. In one case, a union-managed pension plan was "advised" by a counselor—at this writing a resident abroad, busy avoiding extradition back to the United States to face trial on grand jury indictments—who put most of the fund's money into private loans. Out of such loans, he collected the finders' fees that enabled him to leave the country and to live well in nations which have no provision for mutual swapping of wanted men.

Another cause of near-bankruptcy was brought out by Manuel Cohen, Chairman of the Securities and Exchange Commission under Presidents John F. Kennedy and Lyndon Johnson. Testifying on April 27, 1970, before the Subcommittee on Fiscal Policy of the Joint Economic Committee, Mr. Cohen noted:

I am particularly concerned at indications that the so-called performance fad has spread from other types of investment media to administrators and managers of pension funds, whether private or administered by insurance companies. While short-term trading may have its place for certain types of investors . . . there are serious questions as to the appropriateness of such activity for those entrusted with the savings of people whose investment goals are measured in decades rather than weeks or months and who may have little or no control over the timing of their retirement. The current "bear" market may already have left, in its wake, disappointment and worse for recent retirees.

Dr. Roger F. Murray, executive vice-president and chairman of the CREF Finance Committee, Teachers Insurance and Annuity Association and College Retirement and Equities Fund, told the same Subcommittee in answer to a question regarding pension investment in company stock: "I think it is undesirable when the individual is dependent on the future of that enterprise for employment continuity and future contributions to his retirement benefits. He should not also be relying for his asset, for the support of his pension plan, on the same enterprise. I do not say this about profit-sharing plans which perform a different function, but for a pension program it seems to me undesirable that a significant fraction of the fund should be invested in the employer's securities."

START WITH AN OVERALL LONG-RANGE PLAN

What assets are usable for retirement? Mrs. Betty S. Martin, Director of the Women's Division of the Institute of Life Insurance, notes that:

 . . . basically, it's a matter of only three simple steps.

1. What Are Your Resources? Where will your bits and pieces come from? List all the financial assets you can count on after retirement. Some, like your social security or company pension, will be quite obvious; others you might miss thinking about. It's a good idea to make certain you include everything.

2. *What Will Each Provide—In Cash?—In Income?* Some of these answers are readily available, for example, the amount you have in bonds or your savings account. For others, like the exact amount of income you may expect from Social Security, or the exact cash values in your life insurance, you would do well to get help in your figuring from experts in each area, your local Social Security office and your life insurance agent.

3. *How Will You Use Them?* Once you have a clear picture of your assets, you will be ready to decide which to use for income, which to keep as cash for emergencies and which to keep for family protection.

This is an important step in arranging your financial picture for retirement and your decisions may not be easy. First, you'll probably want to do some thinking about your needs for income, for emergency cash and for protection. This will help you see which assets to use for which purpose. You will probably also want to take into consideration the allocation that would be best for husband and wife together and for either partner alone.

It is at this point, too, that couples think about striking a balance in their retirement income between fixed, guaranteed dollars and those with varying values.

Let us read an exchange of correspondence between an investment professional and Harriet and Walter, a couple that set out a few years in advance of retirement to plan a smooth transition from pre- to post-retirement investment tactics.

From: Investment Counselor
To: Harriet and Walter

As I see it, planning for an affluent retirement breaks into two phases with a slower, smaller transition between them.

In the first phase, a buildup of capital is the objective. It is well to remember that if your stake should be lost by trying too hard in go-go stocks or by any other way of attempting to make it in a big hurry, then such a stake is not easily replaced.

Later on, we will phase out that activity for income-producing investments.

Between those two phases, let's transition slowly. A quick switchover might be unadvisable.

From: Walter

To: Investment Counselor

You mention a slow transition as retirement age approaches. Wouldn't it be better to get all the growth we can right up to retirement itself? Seems to us that we might achieve larger capital that way on which to earn income.

From: Investment Counselor

To: Harriet and Walter

The soundest way to get somewhere quickly is not always the fast way. Your capital consists of more than merely cash in the bank. There is the value of your home, for example, long paid for and worth much more than what you paid. You want to move, on retirement, to a sun climate. Will you be able to sell that house in a hurry? Do you know what you wish to accomplish with the proceeds of such a sale? Will you buy a new home elsewhere? Invest the money? Use part for a condominium purchase, part to produce income? Such decisions should be mulled slowly.

Not all investments you can make would be as easily sold as stocks and mutual funds. We should think in terms of one or more of these growth vehicles:

(1) Stocks of good corporations with future potential.

(2) Mutual funds aimed at capital appreciation (but not necessarily at in-out stock-market trading to produce it; such funds tend to be winners one year, losers the next).

(3) Real estate with secure, increasing rentals.

(4) The remodel-resell property market in which you can sometimes find rundown houses at distress prices, remodel to the level of the neighborhood, and resell at a capital gain.

With $20,000 available you should not spread yourself thinly among all of these. But all should be considered.

Next I want you to develop a statement of net worth.

A balance sheet or net-worth statement tells how much you own, free and clear of debt and encumbrance.

In one column, list everything you own: home, cash, paid-up

insurance policies, any debts owed to you. The works. Head the list "assets."

Call the next column "liabilities." In it put down long-term debt if any, accounts you owe to stores and the like contingent debts (as, for example, if you co-signed a note), and other things you owe or which detract from your list of assets.

Total the numbers in each list. Subtract the smaller—in your case liabilities are less—from the larger. The result is your net worth.

FORMULAS ARE NO SUBSTITUTE FOR JUDGMENT

Since the days when alchemists tinkered and blended in an effort to find the Philosophers' Stone which would transmute dross and base metals into shining gold, mankind has clung to a belief that somewhere, there exists a formula for growing rich without effort or the exercise of judgment. One of the formulas thus proposed is labeled dollar cost averaging.

It calls for an investor to purchase the same dollar amount of a stock or a mutual fund at stated intervals. The rationale is that he will be able to purchase more shares during a declining period of the market, fewer when prices are soaring, and that the average price should be one which will generally show a profit. Statistical studies have been made to show that if an investor had done this steadily for ten or twenty years, using selected funds or stocks, he would have fared well.

The plan—like other statistical ways to get rich—has flaws and faults. One is that the vehicles to which it is applied are picked by hindsight; they are stocks or mutuals which always snap back after a sharp decline. The overall market often does this. But you can't count upon any stock or any particular fund doing so every time.

U.S. Steel is the biggest company of its kind in the world. Despite essentially sound management, the stock of Big Steel has steadily gone down from its 1960 high of 108 to a price of 25 on the day when this was written in late 1971, eleven years later. A loss would have been the unenviable lot of any retirement-minded investor who practiced dollar cost averaging in the stock of U.S. Steel.

Ditto some of the hottest go-go mutual funds of a few years ago. Earlier, we looked at Enterprise Fund. In 1963, net-asset value of Enterprise Fund was $10.93 per share. At the same time of year—end of the third quarter—it sank to $8.35 in 1969, then to $5.80 in 1970. During the first half of 1971, stock prices were generally up. Enterprise rose only to $6.71, a price recoup smaller than the general market enjoyed. Dollar cost averaging would not have been a happy experience in Enterprise, despite the fact that until 1968 it had been one of the best performers among mutuals and during one year outperformed all others.

Averaging is no substitute for intelligent selection of investments nor for managing them regularly so that needed changes can be made on time.

Moreover, dollar averaging, with its inflexible emphasis on regular investment of stated amounts, does not take into account the fact that a retirement planner might not have the right amount available on the right day of each month or quarter.

IF SELF-EMPLOYED, LOOK INTO KEOGH

The Keogh law permits self-employed people to put aside portions of income toward retirement. The money is exempt from taxes—for a time; the proceeds are taxed later when drawn out, presumably at lower tax rates expected to apply when actual retirement arrives.

Insurance Annuities Plan   A Keogh plan can be set up to use insurance annuities. You should seriously consider this if you believe that the efforts to contain our raging inflation will succeed (I don't). But if you feel inflation may well get worse (as I believe), then you should be leery of any plan based upon fixed dollars without any fixation of the purchasing power of those dollars.

Mutual Fund Plan   You can arrange your Keogh through mutual fund purchases. Some funds perform well in certain types of market but come unsprung in markets which place emphasis on other investing values. You can't stick a pin in a list and buy whatever mutual fund the pin hits. Study the funds carefully, re-reading Chapter 4.

Bank Trusteeship   Or you can structure your self-employed retirement plan around a bank trustee. You face a problem here that is more difficult than choosing a mutual fund wisely. Bank trust officers are not of equal ability, nor do they operate as resultfully in all kinds of markets. In that respect the bank trust department is like the mutual fund management team. But unlike the mutual management, a bank's results are not easy to find; no public statistics attest to them so that you can choose among trust departments as you would among mutual funds.

A WITHDRAWAL PLAN

Under a withdrawal plan, a retirement planner spends some years accumulating a package of investments to make his senior years secure. Then he spends part of his capital, if needed, to obtain a set income which might be bigger than the income generated by his investments. The following was written for investors by a mutual fund which offers shareholders withdrawal privileges:

> An investor who has acquired shares of the fund that have a value at the current offering price of at least $5,000 . . . may upon request . . . have sufficient shares of the fund automatically redeemed at regular intervals to provide payment to him of $50 or more so as to receive a check a month.
>
> Under this plan, the investor's shares are deposited with a bank as agent for the shareowner, who signs instructions to the bank specifying the amount of the check to be received each month (or quarter as desired). . . . With the bank's approval, payments may be revised at any time by the shareholder.

Note this about the plan: If the amount of the checks received under a check-each-month plan of the type described above exceeds the amount of the dividends credited to the account, the payments will constitute depletion of capital. And as the fund redeems shares for you under this sort of plan, you might find that you have incurred a taxable capital gain if they were bought at a lower price, or a tax loss deductible from income under some circumstances if you paid more for the shares than the cash-up price at the time they were redeemed.

You can use the plan with any kind of stock as well. Instruct your broker to pay you out of dividend income where possible and to sell a share here or there to make up the steady income where dividend accrual isn't sufficient. (Whether your broker is willing to do this is a matter you will have to settle in conversation with the firm that buys and sells securities for you.)

Or you can put your dividend checks into a special account. Withdraw from this monthly. If there is not enough money, sell a share of stock or more if needed. Be aware that commissions charged by brokerage houses are proportionally larger on small transactions such as this than when bigger round-lot amounts are involved.

It is not as easy to sell off a chunk of property as a share of stock. But you can do this, too, under some circumstances, as where a large number of small parcels are involved or several units of a condominium.

Chapter 11

HOW WILL WALL STREET
WORK TOMORROW?

I t is a pretty picture (as far as
it goes) and may be a true visualization of what trading will be
in 1980. The New York Stock Exchange issued this statement
September 1, 1970, bearing the by-line of Dr. William C. Freund,
Vice-President and Economist and Chairman of the Long-Range
Planning Committee of the Big Board:

> You'll still telephone your broker to place a buy or sell
> order for a security listed on the New York Stock Ex-
> change. And the trade will still be made in the Ex-
> change's two-way auction market. But little else may be
> the same in the securities industry a decade or so from
> now.
>
> Late in the trading day sometime in the 1980's, you
> may call your broker and place a buy or sell order for
> 100 (or maybe 10,000) shares of a listed stock. That
> order, if I'm right, will make history.
>
> It'll put the Big Board over the 60-million share level
> for a peak day for the first time during a year when the
> average daily volume hits 36 million.
>
> As I see the picture developing in the future, instead

of going through as many as 66 steps (many of them by hand) your order will be processed almost totally by automation—in virtually seconds.

By 1975, for example, your broker will probably punch in the order on a desk-top computer terminal right while you're on the phone. (Some have already been installed.)

Automatically, your order will be routed to a computer at the Exchange, which will record it and pass it on to the broker on the trading floor for execution in the two-way auction market.

The familiar looseleaf specialist book at the trading post, too, will be replaced by computer-driven television consoles being pilot-tested this fall.

And following execution, computers at the Exchange, your broker, the clearing house and the transfer agent—all linked together, and triggered by the trade—will check the whole transaction for errors, issue you written confirmation, enter your name on your broker's records as a stockholder, and settle the account between the buying and selling brokers.

By 1980, even more dramatic electronic systems than we can visualize today may also be in place—improving the efficiency of the trading operation.

Paperwork will be all but eliminated.

. . . No one can predict, of course, whether volume will be on an up cycle or down in any particular year. But we can project a possible trend line around which volume should fluctuate. If 1980 is an average year, the average daily volume should be about 27 million. If it is an off year, about 18 million. But, if it's a banner year, volume could rise to an average of 36 million shares a day.

This may seem like wishful thinking, since volume averaged less than 11 million shares a day during the first half of 1970. But, remember, volume averaged less than a third of this 10 years ago.

In light of these predicted changes, the Exchange's Long-Range Planning Committee has initiated more than 300 study projects ranging over our entire operation and

probing such things as how to make investing more con
venient so more people can share in our nation's growth

THE PASSING OF EMPHASIS ON
SMALL INVESTORS

One of the things not mentioned in Dr. Freund's statement but
which will be a feature of Wall Street tomorrow is decreasing
emphasis on small investors. In the 1950's and early 1960's the
New York Stock Exchange directed hardhitting sales efforts toward bringing back to stock ownership the small investors who
had deserted the market after the debacle of 1929–1932. The
campaign was notably successful. The ranks of shareowners
swelled to five million, to eight million, ten million, twelve, eight
een, twenty, finally to over thirty million. Then conditions and
emphasis changed. It appears certain that the thrust of future
brokerage sales efforts will not be on the small investor. Larger
game has come into the sights of the Big Board members.

These are the institutions, billions of dollars strong and requiring less scattered sales effort to generate enormous orders
such as millions of individual investors acting in concert could
not produce. Together, they owned 39 percent of all listed stocks
in 1970. The proportion is probably higher now, although no
research into the subject was taken following the Securities and
Exchange Commission's monumental *Institutional Investor Study*.
Institutions proved to be faster on the draw than ordinary individual investors; New York Stock Exchange figures indicated in
April, 1971, that they accounted for 70 percent of an average
day's trading activity.

A single cohesive group of clients, possessed of 39 percent of
stocks and swinging these so actively that they made 70 percent
of the waves, is a better group for cultivation than 30 million
spread-out average investors dealing in 100-share lots of stock—
often smaller—and located along highways and byways where
a large sales force is needed to reach and service them. Con-
tinuation of emphasis on institutions and de-emphasis of efforts
toward smaller investors can certainly be expected.

In 1970 and 1971, brokerage firms by the dozen were going

under. When one of the largest folded, the New York Stock Exchange community looked about to see which surviving entities might be able to service the widespread retail operations of this dying firm. Five firms were singled out as having sufficient financial power to do the job. Four of the five, it turned out, looked on retail investment brokerage as Tiffany's might consider a proposal that it service the jewelry departments of Woolworth. The fifth, emphasizing both retail and institutional business, took over the ailing giant.

Not only has Wall Street turned away from the average investor, but also he in turn has come to look with a less rosy view on the investment world that took away so many of his chips in 1969 and 1970. One disillusioned investor said to me during the market upswing of the summer of 1971: "My father lost his shirt in 1929 and 1932. He warned me to stay away from stock speculation. I didn't listen—who ever does listen to parental advice? And so I took a bath just as he did. It wouldn't have been so bad a bath if I'd stuck to blue-chip stocks. Something like a team of tractors would be required to get me back into a brokerage board room again."

William McChesney Martin, former Federal Reserve Board Chairman and author of a plan for reforming Wall Street, noted in a talk before the New York Financial Writers Association on November 23, 1971: "There are all sorts of people that I run into that don't want to buy stock at all any more. . . . There is a necessity, if we're going to have 'people's capitalism' and . . . the volume of securities owners that I think we need and will have in the next twenty years in this country, to reestablish the integrity of markets in a way that we don't have today."

TIGHTER REGULATION

Speculative abuses prior to the 1929–1932 bear market forced formation of the Securities and Exchange Commission and brought into being the concept that Wall Street, in performing a public service, must be amenable to the public interest. Although speculative abuses of the bull market preceding the 1969–1970 decline were in many ways different from those of the twenties, they are nevertheless bringing in their train tighter regulation.

The Securities and Exchange Commission has taken the lead and its less lenient attitude can be seen in a daily series of clampdown operations. Out of it all will come an investing climate safer for individual investors in the seventies.

Part of the SEC effort has been directed toward more uniform accounting rules, so that some of the "earnings" and other bookkeeping tricks practiced in the late days of the bull market of the sixties will not be repeated. But reform in this area comes slowly. The profession of accounting is unwilling to agree on many things and their corporate employers wish to retain as much latitude as possible in order to build "values" tomorrow. The effort to change freewheeling practices with the books will, I believe, be ultimately successful. But it will not come in a hurry. It may take a decade or more to effect compulsory accounting uniformity.

Other regulatory efforts have been toward enforcing existing rules and making capital requirements work, advertising claims believable, and prospectus notations in total line with all facts. During one six-week period, the following article in the SEC's *News Digest* and in other publications of the financial press told the story of tighter regulatory effort which should make Wall Street a safer place for future small investors:

"(Chairman William J.) Casey told the IBA that the Commission intends to codify and announce soon an additional procedure—summary review of registration statements—which will entail notification to the company that limited processing has been done and the registrant will get only the comments resulting from this review. He said that the Commission is also considering more effective use of transmittal letters covering the initial filing and of cover letters accompanying amendments to help speed up this process.

"Casey also told the meeting that the Commission is on the way to greater clarity and certainty in the rules governing the sale of restricted stock."

IMPROVED METHODS OF STOCK BUYING AND SELLING

Two ways have been proposed to improve methods of buying and selling stock. The "Martin Report" was authored by William

McChesney Martin, ex-NYSE President and ex-Chairman of the Board of Governors of the Federal Reserve System, widely known and universally respected in the financial community. Martin tackled the tie-ups, hang-ups, inefficiencies, and abuses of the existing system. He proposed a super-New York Stock Exchange embracing the whole country and many securities. The Martin Report is—as I write this and, I suspect, for a long time to come —in the discussion stage. Before its proposals can be put into effect, the brokerage industry will have to agree and bring into the area of agreement such segments as the mutual funds and other institutions that have billion-dollar interests in how their investments are bought and sold.

Already operational is the second solution to the mess of hung-up security deliveries, slowed transactions, and the controversial specialist setup. This solution, backed by forces as strong as those behind the NYSE-sponsored Martin Report, is called NASDAQ. It is the baby of the National Association of Securities Dealers and is fully computerized.

While opposing forces of the New York Stock Exchange and the National Association of Securities Dealers argued merits of their respective plans, SEC Chairman Casey stressed the need to quickly provide—through one or a combination of both—faster and more efficient securities trading. He told the Investment Bankers Association:

> Among steps, I can see these clearly right now, (1) a combination of composite tape and recall box to bring all transactions out into the open to make prices, volume and quotes in all markets available to all, (2) a set of rules which will bring all existing market makers into a system designed to maximize liquidity, make competition work to narrow spreads and assure all investors that they can have an opportunity to participate at the best prices available and (3) broadened public representation in the governance of the securities markets.
>
> Progress has been made in modernizing clearance methods but more is needed. I believe that automated trading can be carried to automated clearing and settlement. We can and must establish a course which will take us in a few years to a nationwide system of securi-

ties transfer and payment. (SEC *News Digest,* December 2, 1971)

In addition to how and where securities are traded in the new decade ahead, Wall Street must settle who will do the trading. The New York Stock Exchange has battled to prevent institutions—already members of regional exchanges—from joining its club, where they hope to be able to execute their own orders without payment of commissions to NYSE brokerage members, and in the process save money for pensioners, mutual fund shareowners, and other fiduciary clients. The NYSE will probably lose this struggle.

One interesting development has taken an old commodity exchange into the trading of stocks along with soybean and wheat futures. Stock "futures" in the form of Put and Call options will be traded on an organized exchange, to the advantage of both writers and buyers of these options. As explained in a brochure:

The Chicago Board of Trade believes it has developed this concept to the point of providing an option marketplace so much improved in structure that it comes close to representing a distinct new investment medium. With formation of the Chicago Board Options Exchange, the Board of Trade is creating a separate new securities exchange to actually conduct the market. The CBOE will have facilities adjoining the Board of Trade's and will look to it for many professional and technical services. Although there is likely to be a considerable overlap in membership between the Board of Trade and the CBOE, the new Exchange will be a separate entity with its own membership, its own governing board and rules and regulatory policies adhering to securities industry practice.

Trading will be conducted on an auction basis at posts on the CBOE floor with orders coming to the posts from the wire facilities of member firms. For each security dealt in, a "board broker" will be designated by the Exchange to assume responsibility for orders that are directed to him. There are expected to be, in addition, several competing "market makers" in each security who will share responsibilities for maintenance of a fair and orderly market. All transactions will be reported promptly on an

Exchange tape. Trades will be processed and settlements made through an Options Clearing Corp., which will function in much the same manner as the Chicago Board of Trade Clearing Corp.

During an initial trial period, the CBOE will deal in call options alone, starting with markets in perhaps 20 to 50 widely held, actively traded, listed stocks. Trading in puts and option trading in additional stocks will be introduced as operating experience is gained.

The single most important new feature of the Chicago Board option market is a secondary market in which options originated on the CBOE can thereafter be freely traded. This innovation sets Chicago Board options totally apart from the OTC options of today which have virtually no resalability.

MUTUAL FUNDS ARE CHANGING

Finally, one change in the stock-market arena that will make life less scary for everyone, is that the go-go operators of the recent past will disappear entirely from the mutual-fund scene. That is not to say that all management will be wise in the future, but it will be a long time before the speculative approach that lost so many millions of investors' dollars will flourish again.

Chapter 12

CAN INVESTORS
AVOID PAPA BEAR?

A new generation of invest-
ment people came along in the sixties. They had no inhibiting
memories of past down markets nor did they know the dictum
that the arts of economics and investing can be summed up in
Friedman's single sentence: "There is no free lunch."

There won't be any free lunch in the years to come. Excesses
must be paid for, no matter the economic climate or the euphoria
of those who predict future happenings. In Chapter 2, we postu-
lated a probable economic frame of reference for the years ahead.
This called for a period of economic stagnation and decline,
followed by a fresh boom, but no early return to wild speculation such as was seen in the later years of the sixties.

Given such a development, is there need to worry about future bear markets? Will the return of sobriety to Wall Street and
to the Main Streets on which so many burned investors live bring
about a hoped-for freedom from further sizable decline?

There will still be upswings and downswings in the overall
course of stock prices. Some of these will be little and can be
ignored as factors in formulating investing judgment. Some of
them will be big, however—big enough to call bull markets and

bear markets—and it is reasonable to expect that the bear swings of the future will be able to destroy capital as effectively as did the bear swings of the past. Unless, of course, an investor knows how to spot them before they arrive or while they are still small, and also knows the steps he should take to protect himself—even enhance capital—during the bear movements which are wrecking less perceptive stock buyers.

HOW TO SPOT STOCK-MARKET TRENDS

In recent years some new methods of assessing market swings have been developed, and these can be usefully applied by any interested investor.

Secondaries In *Barron's* magazine, November 29, 1971, Robert Koehler, market analyst of the Trust Department of First National Bank of Chicago, unveiled a study in using secondary offerings as an indicator of coming changes in market trend. A secondary is an offering of stock from a shareowner or institution, in a block large enough to call for marketing through an underwriting rather than the normal avenues of stock selling. Secondary offerings are a matter of record; leading financial publications carry news of them as announced.

In constructing his indicator, Mr. Koehler employed moving averages. To make such an average, an analyst chooses a length of time, then averages the figures during that period. The average "moves" when he re-computes it by dropping the last digit and adding the newest one. For example, in a ten-day moving average of the numbers 1, 2, 3, 4, 5, 6, 7, 8, 9, and 10, the first average would be their sum, 55, divided by 10, or 5.5. On the eleventh day, the digit "1" representing the first period would be dropped, and the digit "11" representing the newest period, added. The new sum would be 65, the new moving average number 6.5. Moving averages are used frequently in constructing indexes; the reason is to avoid excessive up-down movements which raw, unadjusted figures might give.

Mr. Koehler explained:

> The negative impact of an increasing number of secondaries on stock price levels—the so-called Secondary Syndrome—is commonly explained in two ways: (1) second-

aries contribute directly to the supply of stock available, and (2) a large number of such offerings may indicate a shift in preference away from stock and into cash—a trend that will ultimately result in decreased demand. A systematic study of secondary activity over the past 11 years offers evidence that it does indeed relate to future market trends.

An analysis of the moving monthly averages for both the number of secondaries issued and their total value has shown each to display a good lead relationship to major stock price trends. However, the average number of secondaries offered consistently proved to be a more reliable indicator than did the total value concept. Building upon this, an optimal investment strategy was developed from the historical relation between the number offered and subsequent market trends. It indicated a selling point when a three-month moving average rose above 24 offerings per month and a buying area when they fell below eight. . . . these indicators have proved remarkably accurate in calling the major bull and bear markets of the past decade. Specifically, a buy-and-hold strategy from March 1960 until September 1970 would have yielded a total return (pretax capital gains—plus reinvested dividends minus commissions) of 110.2%. If during the same period long and short positions were taken on the Dow as determined by the system at the indicated action prices, a total return of 313.2% would have been realized—nearly three times that of a buy-and-hold strategy.

The superior return of this system is attributable to the fact that of the seven signals given over the past 11 years, each showed a substantial profit. Hindsight reveals that each was near what is now recognized as major turning points in the trend of stock prices. Moreover, the system boasts an unusually consistent record of distinguishing major bull and bear trends from more intermediate and transitory price movements.

Koehler's paper indicated the buy-sell signals given during the decade under study (Table 7):

TABLE 7. BUY-SELL SIGNALS

Date of signal	Market action	Moving monthly avg. of secondaries[a]	Action DJIA level[b]
Sept. 1960	Buy	5.0	580.4
Sept. 1961	Sell	29.7	703.9
Aug. 1962	Buy	7.0	579.0
Apr. 1965	Sell	25.3	918.0
Oct. 1966	Buy	5.7	791.6
June 1968	Sell	26.3	883.0
May 1970	Buy	7.7	683.5
Apr. 1971	Sell	24.3	907.8

[a] Three-month moving average.
[b] One month after 3-month period.

"Most Active" Stocks In another *Barron's* article, an indicator was proposed based upon strength or weakness among the weekly list of "most active" stocks. In the April 28, 1969, issue, F. R. West noted that the list of most-active New York Stock Exchange stocks made an effective market barometer. The top twenty stocks, he noted, while comprising only 1 percent of total number of issues, generated 20 percent of volume of shares traded. Using, not a single week's trading, but a minimum of three weeks' study—and taking longer periods as more meaningful—he considered "par" on the upside for three weeks as 60 (20 × 3). He noted minus 60 (−20 × 3) as "par" for the downside. His report continued:

> If one were relying solely on the behavior of the "most actives" to spotlight bottom reversals after lengthy and sizable declines (an unlikely and illogical approach considering the many useful companion tools available), the experience beginning with the 1962 bottom tells us that the oscillator should react to depths approaching or exceeding minus 50 following lengthy, accelerating declines that terminate with a convulsive climax as in 1962 and 1966. In the case of lengthy, drifting declines that bottom out quietly, as in 1968, the oscillator should have dropped well into minus territory before reversing its trend for a number of weeks while the price level was still declining or beginning to flatten out.

Under either of the foregoing ground rules stocks can be bought. Subsequently, to confirm the validity of the advance, the oscillator should rise to plus 40 or higher and make successive thrusts above the plus 40 line, as it did in 1962–1965, 1966–1967 and 1968. In 1964, while the oscillator fluctuated in its usual manner and remained below the plus 40 level, it made a series of ascending peaks in the plus 33–37 range, which also was indicative of underlying strength.

By contrast, a warning light flashes when the "most active" made a series of descending peaks against concurrently rising stock prices. Thus, on October 20, 1961, the Dow closed at 705.62 and the oscillator stood at plus 38. Five weeks later, on November 24, the average had reached 732.60, the peak of the 1960–1961 advance. By that time the oscillator had slipped to plus 26, a definite warning signal. The market then sagged and recovered: on March 16, 1962, the Dow closed at 722.77, less than 10 points below the actual top of a 155-point upswerve. The oscillator also had reacted and recovered, but on March 16 was no better than plus 13. The following week the 1962 break began. The period of deterioration of strength in the "most actives" had lasted 21 weeks (from October 20 to March 16).

Speculative Fever Index   Professionals in the investment field often refer to a market as "overbought" (in which case they expect a short-term decline) or "oversold" (a condition from which they look for a short-range price rebound). "Overbought" and "oversold" are hard to define. One way to determine their presence is an index composed of the Dow Jones Industrial Average of blue chips and an index of low-priced stocks. The two are employed together by dividing the level of the low-priced stock index each week by the level of the DJIA. The result gives a Speculative Fever Reading, whose purpose is to tell the degree of interest in cat and dog stocks (a derogatory term for low-priced issues) vis-à-vis blue chips. Here's how I described the Reading in my May, 1969, "Technician's Post" column in *Investment Sales Monthly:*

When the ratio which results from this computation is on

the rise, an observer can safely say that low-priced stocks are relatively more in favor than blue-chip stocks at the moment. The word "relative" is important, since both indexes can be rising, with one going up much more rapidly than the other. It is their relationship to each other that the Speculative Fever Index measures, not the absolute level, or even the absolute trend, of either index.

It has been found that when this index makes new peaks, the market might well be in an overbought condition. For example, during 1968 the Speculative Fever Index made two sharply-rising tops. In the year's first months it zoomed rapidly. The sharp and hurtful decline in the overall market, which came after this overbought signal, is still a painful memory to many investors.

Then came the "peace speech" of President Johnson and the sudden spring rise of 1968. During this rise the Speculative Fever Index, which had bottomed at 37.8 in the middle of April, shot swiftly up to a new high at 47.6 in the third week of June. After that came the summer doldrums of the stock market, when nothing moved very much.

The indicator then dropped irregularly to a level around 39.6, from which bottom a spirited autumn rise was soon underway in the overall market.

The Speculative Fever Index can be read as a series of tabulated numbers. It will give exactly the same sort of reading that it indicates when charted on paper. But as is the case with many technical tools, its use is simplified by making the index visual.

NYSE Seats   The price of a seat (membership) on the New York Stock Exchange has been taken by some analysts as an indicator of market health. Their rationale is that when things are going well, prospective members bid higher to obtain membership in the NYSE, and existing members who consider selling raise their prices because they feel that the seat has higher value. Conversely, during down markets and periods when those with an inside view look for declining overall price levels, the would-be buyer and prospective seller of an exchange seat lower the levels of bid and ask.

It is not so much the absolute price as the trend of rising or lessening prices for a seat which give signals of trouble when bear markets might be around the corner or opportunity when the makings of a new bull movement are being assembled.

During the fifties, prices of an NYSE seat rose irregularly, dropping in the 1958 bear market, but rising sharply after it and tumbling to indicate the 1962 bear market that shaved so much from share valuations. Seat bid-ask prices moved upward, leveling off during the 1966 bear trend and resuming a climb until they took a fall in 1969. The price fell still more in 1970.

The indicator value of a seat price is more confirmatory than prophetic—it tends to tell the observer that a decline which is starting is likely to be a serious one rather than a casual reaction, and it gives confirmation to a new uptrend. Figures on NYSE seat prices are found in the financial press.

Bank Interest Rate Changes   The bank interest (discount) rate of the Federal Reserve is not a precise indicator which infallibly rings bells when something big is about to occur in either direction. But the timing of rate changes sometimes forewarns of a coming stock-market movement. It works better on the bear side than in foretelling bull markets. As such, observance of rate changes is a worthwhile secondary tool for watching market trends.

The record for the period 1959–1970 follows.

In 1959, the Federal Reserve steadily upped the rate, starting at 2½ percent—a going figure for those times of easier money— and increasing all the way to 3½ and 4 percent late in the year. The latter figure, low by comparison with numbers that came later, was high at the time.

Stocks tumbled in 1960.

The rate indicator failed to warn of the 1962 bear market. During 1963, 1964, and 1965, rates were gradually upped until they reached 4½ percent in late 1965. A hurtful bear market appeared in 1966.

In 1968, rates rose steadily, to 4½ percent, 5 percent, 5½ percent. Then in 1969, stock prices fell out of bed. The Fed continued to apply money tautness during 1969; its rate that troubled year rose to 6 percent. The bear market continued into 1970, when rates were reduced to 5¾ and 5½ percent.

Stock Group Index Observance of what happens in a number of industry averages is of value in foretelling a coming major market move, or confirming that a beginning new trend is likely to be of major importance. We base such an index upon the 35 groups reported every week in *Barron's*. You could use industry groups of any statistical service. The index is compiled as a "cumulative differential."

Example: Assume for an opening week that 14 of the 35 groups went up, one was even, and 20 declined. Ignoring the standoff group, the difference between 20 losers and 14 gainers is a −6. That becomes the starting figure of the index.

If next week there is a plurality of 20 gainers, then to cumulate this differential, add +20 to −6 and come up with a figure of +14. That is the second week's level. The computation sounds complicated but in practice it takes only minutes.

These numbers are plotted across chart paper and read in standard technical chart reading fashion. Signals are rendered by the upside breaking of an important overhead point at which previous advances stopped—this would give a bullish signal—or downside break from previous major support to render a bearish signal.

The rationale behind this indicator is that for a market to have a valid trend, there must be wide follow-through of many industry groups, rather than narrow price movement in a few stocks. The latter kind of action can force up a price index even though only a minority of stocks are in rising trends. But it takes broad action by many stocks to produce a goodly number of industry groups that appear in bullish trends when plotted out on chart paper.

Our records for this indicator covering a hectic seven-year period, 1965–1971, show these buy and sell signals for the overall market:

Aug. 7, 1965, buy	June 3, 1968, buy
Dec. 13, 1965, sell	Feb. 17, 1969, sell
Dec. 13, 1966, buy	Sept. 28, 1970, buy
Oct. 23, 1967, sell	Aug. 27, 1971, sell

Option Activity Ratio An indicator based upon speculative activity was proposed by Martin E. Sweig, Assistant Professor of Economics and Finance, Bernard M. Baruch College of the City University of New York, in a November 30, 1970, article in *Barron's*.

He noted the old Theory of Contrary Opinion—a hoary Wall Street adage that one should always distrust and act against majority views—which would indicate that when there is a great deal of option activity, then speculative feeling is high and speculative excess probable. During the decade preceding publication of his theory, Dr. Sweig said, Put and Call activity normally ran around one percent of the trading volume on the New York Stock Exchange. The range was between 0.5 percent and 1.3 percent of volume of shares traded. Thus, he reasoned, an Option Activity Ratio (OAR) somewhere between those figures would be normal, while a lower activity would denote extreme pessimism and a higher one extreme optimism.

He continued:

> Unfortunately, it is not so easy to measure speculative enthusiasm. It is always possible that an atypical reading for a week or two might be attributable to random factors and thus prove meaningless for predictive purposes. In order to nullify the effect of temporary aberrations in the Option Activity Ratio, it was necessary to compile a moving average of the figure. Such a moving average of the weekly OAR was calculated on a 10-week basis for the past decade.
>
> The 10-week moving average of the Option Activity Ratio was then carefully examined for "atypical" behavior. The examination produced the following rules:
>
> (1) When both the 10-week moving average and the weekly reading of the OAR rise above 1.25, it is likely that speculation is rampant and stocks should be sold.
>
> (2) When both the 10-week moving average and the weekly reading of the OAR fall below 0.75, it is likely that speculative enthusiasm is relatively low and thus stocks should be bought.
>
> Using the above rules, five signals have been given in the past decade. . . .
>
> Prior to 1970, there were five major turning points in stock prices in the decade; namely, the peaks of 733 on the Dow Jones Industrial Average (weekly close) in

November 1961, 989 in February 1966 and 985 in November 1968; and the troughs of 539 in June 1962, and 744 in October 1966. With the exception of the 1966 peak, the OAR clearly called these turns within a reasonable degree of error (for those interested in staying with the primary trend—not for fast traders).

The signal with the greatest deviation from the extreme point in the market cycle was the sell signal in 1961, which occurred 31 weeks and 48 Dow points prior to the November peak. . . . The 1962 and 1966 troughs and the 1968 peak weekly Dow Jones prices were missed by only one, two and four weeks, respectively, by the OAR.

The Keran Model   The turn signals discussed above are relatively easy to compile and understand. Not so those from an ambitious "model" of the market put together by Michael W. Keran, Economist and Assistant Vice-President of the Federal Reserve Bank of St. Louis. For those who understand and like complicated mathematics, Dr. Keran's method is explained briefly in the excerpt below from his monumental "Expectations, Money and the Stock Market" which appeared in the January, 1971, issue of the *Review* of the St. Louis Federal Reserve Bank. It has been reprinted in full (Reprint Series No. 63) by the St. Louis Fed and can be had on request from its research department.

The theory of stock price determination has always been clear in concept but weak in application. Conceptually, the price an individual is willing to pay for an equity share is equal to the discount to present value of both expected future dividends and the discount to present value of the expected stock price at the time of sale. In its simplest form, this relationship can be represented by the following equation:

(1) $$SP_t = \frac{D_{t+1}^e}{(1 + R)} + \frac{D_{t+2}^e}{(1 + R)^2} + \cdots + \frac{D_{t+n}^e}{(1 + R)^n} + \left[\frac{SP_{t+n}^e}{(1 + R)^n}\right]$$

where:

SP_t = Stock Price today—as valued by the individual investor

SP^e = Stock Price expected at time of sale

D_e^{t+n} = Dividends expected

R = Interest Rate expressed in decimal form (8.1% is written as .081)

The value which an individual will place on equities today will rise if dividends are expected to rise or if the stock price is expected to be higher at the date of sale (so-called capital gains). The value an individual attaches to equities today will fall if the interest rate increases, because the rate at which one discounts expected future dividends and capital gains has risen, and consequently the present value is lower.

The above is a brief part of a complicated academic paper. My purpose in including the excerpt here is to record Dr. Keran's "model." In a chart comparing actual and predicted courses of stock prices during the past decade, predicted stock prices began a rise in 1960 slightly prior to the rise in actual averages. The rise peaked during 1961 before prices turned over to become the 1962 bear market. The actual bottom of the 1962 downturn came before the rising indication given by "predicted values of stock price index." The two continued upward to a simultaneous peak during 1965. The 1966 bear trend followed. "Predicted value" of the stock price index did not sink as deep as actual prices, and the two then rose together until a rounding over of predicted values in 1968. The bear market of 1969–1970 followed.

There was close correlation of predicted value and actual price, and an investor with sufficient mathematical knowledge to employ the Keran model should be in an excellent position to predict important future market turns.

SOME INDICATORS CAN'T BE TRUSTED

Inflation   Don't take inflation as a harbinger of a rising stock market. All during the fifties and early years of the sixties, when inflation was gentle, people associated the continuance of inflation with long-range continuance of a rising stock market.

"Rising costs and lessened dollar values have to be offset in some manner by smart money managers," they reasoned. "How better than in common stocks, where the trend is for price of shares to rise and where inflation can also increase corporate profits in dollars if not in real terms?"

For a time this reasoning appeared to work. Then it became apparent that rising inflation, instead of helping corporate profits to grow, was actually putting companies in a bind, caught between costs that rose rapidly and price increases that rose not quite so rapidly and that always seemed to stay a step or two behind wage increases and material costs.

Moreover, although growth theoreticians denied it, dividends constitute a factor—albeit not an overriding one—in the setting of stock prices. Dividends to the income investor are like interest in that, for yield purposes, the rate of inflation must be taken as a factor lessening real return. For example, a 5 percent return in times of no inflation gives the investor five cents real annual income for every dollar invested. If inflation is at a 3 percent rate, his true return is lessened to 2 percent. Inflation thus acted as a two-way brake on stock prices.

Majority Opinion   Distrust majority opinion, *particularly when the opinions come from professionals in Wall Street.* The adage that any majority is always wrong about the course of the stock market applies to advisers, counselors, analysts, and brokerage spokesmen. Some services compile professional opinions; these are worth watching although thousands of advisory sources are in existence and, by their nature, the letters which sample these can look at only a tiny sample. When you consult the majority opinion, take a contrary view. The majority is not always wrong, but it is wrong in a sufficient number of cases to make any consensus suspect.

Government Predictions   Government prophets are the least reliable. Consider this statement regarding inflation made as part of a speech on "The Management of Resumed Expansion" before the Economic Club of Detroit in that city on October 19, 1970, by Dr. Paul W. McCracken, then Chairman of the Council of Economic Advisers. "The program of disinflation is beginning to turn the flank of the price level," Dr. McCracken told his audience and, through wide dissemination of the speech, the nation at large. "The acceleration in the rate of inflation was halted in 1969, and in 1970 monthly increases in the consumer price index have been around a clearly declining trend. In the first quarter of this year, for example, the consumer price index was rising at the rate of 6.3 percent per year; in the second quarter it was

5.8 percent, and the fourth quarter increase will be substantially smaller still."

Not only did inflation fail to halt as predicted, it reached a virulent stage in the months following this speech. Price and wage controls had to be instituted only nine months later in August, 1971, in an effort to curb it. Moreover, "resumed expansion" failed to materialize and the country wallowed in recession during the next twelve months.

Outpourings from Washington economists and seers are politically oriented and paint a picture that the politicians—whether Republican or Democratic—want to have believed. "There is always an eye on the next election," one cynical Congressman told me, "and that holds true whether statements come from figures in politics or from any branch of the Federal government which has to follow the party line of the politicians in power."

STRATEGY FOR A BEAR MARKET

Investors cannot stem the onset of bear tides, but they can use those tides and times to carry them forward.

Earlier, we examined the record of buy and sell signals given for the overall market by our Stock Group Index. These did not coincide with absolute tops and bottoms in the market averages. The signal occasionally came early, more often it flashed after the top or bottom had been made. Yet its value was great. The buy and sell signals indicated by the Stock Group Index came in August, 1965, December, 1965, December, 1966, October 1967, June, 1968, February, 1969, September, 1970, and August, 1971. The tabulation below gives an average type of prices obtainable during the month on General Motors, a bellwether blue-chip stock. During the period, GM's average yearly price declined from 104 to 82¼. This would have given an investor who merely bought and held blue-chip GM a total loss of 21¾ points. *Had he bought and sold GM on bull market–bear signals, his profit would have been 69⅜ points per share,* although one transaction broke even and another resulted in a small loss.

The tabulation below assumes that our investor bailed out of his holding of GM every time the Stock Group Index told him

that the overall market was going to head downward, and sold
short during the down periods.

	Profit	Loss
Aug. 1965, buy 101½		
Dec. 1965, sell 105	3½	
Dec. 1966, buy 70½	34½	
Oct. 1967, sell 81½	11½	
June 1968, buy 81½	Even	Even
Feb. 1969, sell 79½		2
Sept. 1970, buy 71	8½	
Aug. 1971, sell 84⅜	13⅜	

Wise strategy on a sell signal for the overall market calls for:
(1) Sale of all common stocks in the portfolio. Money that
isn't "at work" still works when the stocks into which it might be
exchanged are going down in price relative to dollars.

In July, 1970, I explained this policy to clients of the *Markstein
Letter*:

> A severe Papa Bear market such as this one offers you
> opportunity to become a great deal wealthier than you
> now are . . . a current market debacle could be the big-
> gest opportunity of your lifetime.

> An upturn that comes after a Papa Bear like this is
> usually a big one. At such a time, investors who have
> conserved capital by staying on the market sidelines have
> opportunity to reap very big benefits. I can't promise you,
> of course, that when our indicators do signal a new bull
> market, they will be correct. Nothing in past performance
> guarantees future results. But when the indicators say
> it is time to buy again, I intend to reinvest my personal
> funds and to put machinery in motion for buys in four
> model accounts. I hope that such a course could result
> in a big profit payoff.

> However, people who fritter away capital riding bear
> market prices downward are likely to have limited capi-
> tal with which to participate then. If it turns out that
> the bottom was seen, we will have lost little by our wait.
> If the eventual bottom was not seen, then capital needful
> at the bullish turn will have been wasted.

(2) Purchase of Treasury Bills and bank Certificates of Deposit (three months at a time on Bills, no longer than 30-day maturities on the CD's) with the purpose of maintaining maximum liquidity with minimum risk and minimum tie-up of capital. Buy CD's when their yields appear to be better than yields available on short-term Treasury paper.

(3) Selling short. How much capital you use for shorting—10, 20, 40, or 100 percent—will depend upon the degree of your conviction that things are going badly in the market, and the extent to which you can sleep well with money out at maximum risk. For most of us, I suggest a proportion of 20 to 40 percent short positions, with the remainder in cash or yield-bearing equivalents such as Treasury Bills and bank Certificates of Deposit. As a bear market grows older, the proportion devoted to shorting should become smaller since risks in shorting grow greater, and the proportion in cash and interest-bringing equivalents should become larger.

Chapter 13

REAL ESTATE WAYS
FOR A NEW DECADE

Real estate boomed during the sixties. It was then a play for big investors able to obtain capital in six figures, and preferably in seven- or eight-figure amounts. They had to find, finance, develop, in some circumstances build upon, and eventually peddle to buyers their parcels of land and their piles of bricks, wood, and mortar. Great fortunes were often made in real estate in this manner. Sometimes fortunes were lost. Although a few of the real estate biggies of the 1960's began with small stakes which they increased into big amounts, real estate was essentially a game for the big boys to play. If you sat at their board underfinanced, you could lose fast.

Opportunities will remain in real estate in the seventies and eighties. They are, if anything, enhanced. They're available now for small operators and investors on an ordinary scale, thanks to many changes which have occurred in the structure of real estate. Participation has become simpler as well as cheaper.

THE OPPORTUNITIES

After World War II ended, the rate of births soared. As these boys and girls grew older, their needs ballooned. New homes were built to accommodate the increased needs. Whereas the average home had contained one and a half bedrooms and a single bath, "average" became three bedrooms and two bathrooms. Land was cleared, trees felled, swamps and ditches filled, to make room for this expansion of North America's housing needs.

Then the birth rate declined to a more normal level. Making new houses was no longer the sure road to sudden wealth, although it remained a profitable business.

It is expected that another big wave of births will come shortly. The big crop of post-World War II babies are no longer children. They have grown to maturity, married, and are now having their own children.

Another factor working to make real estate investment a success is the emphasis on restructuring blighted cities. Only now beginning, this program can be expected to increase in scope throughout the decade.

A third factor is the building of entirely new cities, under Federal auspices, in which it is hoped the quality of life will be better than in the overcrowded inner urban cores and the sprawling suburbs of today. This is a field offering more opportunity to wealthy investors than to those possessing moderate capital, and greatest opportunity to corporations which have not only the capital but the staffs of experts to make new dream communities a reality of tomorrow. If you have the resources, look into it.

EASIER WAYS TO GET INTO REAL ESTATE

Real Estate Investment Trusts   Real Estate Investment Trusts are not altogether new, but their widespread availability is a phenomenon of the seventies.

In the August, 1971, *Monthly Review* of the Federal Reserve Bank of New York, Leon Korobow, Chief of the Financial Statistics Division, and Richard J. Gelson, Economist of the New York Fed, examined "Real Estate Investment Trusts: An Appraisal of their Impact on Mortgage Credit":

> The rapid growth of Real Estate Investment Trusts (REITs) during 1968–70 provides another illustration of the ability of financial institutions and markets to make

adaptive changes in the face of severe liquidity pressures and credit scarcities. These investment companies operate under the Real Estate Investment Act of 1960, which exempts the trusts from corporate income and capital gains taxation, provided they pay out nearly all their income. *A fundamental objective of the legislation is to facilitate real estate investment by granting trusts the same tax advantages enjoyed by regulated investment companies, such as mutual funds,* which invest mainly in corporate equities and bonds. The legislation also encourages REITs to seek wide ownership of their shares, thus promoting broad-based participation in the ownership of real estate assets. (Italics supplied.)

. . . To qualify for special tax treatment, REITs must distribute at least 90 percent of their ordinary income to their shareholders, derive not less than 75 percent of their gross income from real estate transactions (e.g., rents, interest on mortgages, and sales of property) and hold at least 75 percent of their assets in the form of real estate loans and property, cash, and Government securities. The shares of a REIT must be issued to no fewer than one hundred persons, and the holdings of five or fewer individuals cannot exceed 50 percent of the total. In addition, REITs must function as investors in, rather than managers of, real estate and they may not hold property primarily for resale. When the trusts so qualify, the income and capital gains they distribute are taxed only when received by their shareholders. These provisions permit the trusts to offer returns that are attractive to investors in the low to moderate income-tax brackets.

Some of the features of Real Estate Investment Trusts are:

(1) They can issue a wide latitude of equity (stock and ownership) or debt (bond) instruments.

(2) They are able to operate across wide geographical areas.

(3) They are not inhibited by rules regarding the kinds of people and companies to whom they can lend, nor the amount to a particular borrower.

(4) Some hold only mortgage notes. Others invest in direct ownership of real estate. Most of the newer trusts prefer to have

some ownership as well as debt since this permits them to participate in profits (if profits accrue).

(5) REIT's have sold to the public both debt (their own
bonds) and stock. They have tried to make an appeal, through
one or the other of these kinds of self-financing, to both investors
interested in hopeful appreciation and those seeking steady income.

Real Estate Limited Partnerships. Equally available for
purchase, although harder to sell if you want to get out, are
limited partnerships in real estate. These escape some of the
regulation that REIT's undergo. They are thus more attractive
to the people who promote real estate investments, but possibly
less so to those who purchase participations.

A typical participation offered units requiring initial investment of $2,500 and additional investment of up to $12,500. Some
of the drawbacks were explained in this prospectus:

> The holding of land for investment is speculative by na-
> ture. The marketability and value of the property at any
> time is dependent upon many factors not subject to the
> Company's control, such as the need for residential hous-
> ing of the kind which might be constructed on the prop-
> erty, the availability of developers or investors of other
> properties in the area, the cost of development, the avail-
> ability and expense of mortgage financing for developers
> and ultimate purchasers, and possible governmental use
> of adjoining properties and the property. In addition the
> company believes that unless changes are obtained in the
> current zoning of the property it would not be practicable
> for developers to build homes on the property, and con-
> sequently the marketability and value of the property
> could be substantially adversely affected. A purchaser
> should realize that it may take several years before the
> Company may be able to sell the property to developers
> interested in developing it on a basis profitable to the
> Company and that, upon any such sale, the Company
> may not receive all the cash proceeds until several years
> after such sale. The profitability, if any, to the Company
> of such sales may depend on the capability and financial

stability of the developers and, in part, on the financial stability of the ultimate purchasers from the developers. Furthermore, there is no assurance that the property can ever be sold at a profit.

. . . Because only a limited number of Units are being sold pursuant to this offering and because of the limited transferability of Units under the Partnership Agreement, it is not expected that any public market will develop for the Units. Accordingly, an investment in the Units cannot be expected to be readily liquidated. Moreover, while the initial amount payable is $2,500 per Unit, the investor will be required to meet possible calls of up to an additional $12,500 per Unit for his interest. Failure to make additional contributions when they are called for may result in loss or substantial depreciation in value of the initial investment. In the event an investor fails to meet promptly such calls for additional contributions, he will remain liable therefore. Furthermore, his interest may be sold in satisfaction of a lien in favor of the Company to the extent of such unpaid calls.

There is a plus side to ownership of limited real estate partnerships. The brochure of one promotion explained it this way:

Tax Shelter—The investment is designed to generate and distribute tax-sheltered income. In addition, each investor's share of annual depreciation is frequently sufficient to reduce his state and Federal taxes on income from other sources. The partnership, as such, is not taxed.

Hedge Against Inflation—Appreciation in property value and pre-planned increases in rent schedules offset inflationary trends.

Limited Liability—Limited partners assume no liability beyond their original financial commitment.

Minimum Investment Required—Usually at least $2,500. Securities regulations may also specify that participants meet income and net worth minimums.

Limited Availability—Real estate investments which satisfy our criteria and meet current needs of an investor are not always available.

These syndicate participations offer opportunities and suffer from pitfalls common to all "tax shelter" partnerships which will be treated in detail in the next chapter.

BIG INCOME MORTGAGE

Say "mortgage" and many bring to mind the villain of a period movie, twirling a long mustache and foreclosing on the ranch of the heroine's father, while a frantic hero gallops up with money to pay the baddie. The word has unfortunate connotations. It should not. Without the institution of mortgage credit, America's housing would exist only in truncated form.

Once mortgage investing was available only to those able to put up five- and six-figure packages of cash. But no more. Now you can invest in mortgages easily.

One way is through purchase of shares of Real Estate Investment Trusts, which put all or nearly all their capital into mortgages. These are often called Mortgage Investment Trusts (MIT's). Investors can purchase in small packages and receive professional management which chooses the mortgages and collects payments. As with common stock mutual funds, MIT and REIT managements are of varying skill despite the collective claim to professionalism, and it is well to check their records. This isn't as easy as with stock mutual funds.

Writing in a research report of Harris, Upham and Co., Analyst Gary L. Wolf enumerated seven characteristics of what he termed "the ideal mortgage trust."

> The best way to summarize the selection process would seem to be the description of an ideal trust. Many trusts . . . have short operating histories. These periods, however inconclusive, should bear evidence of several key factors, namely:
>
> (1) An ability to fund loan commitments within a short time after the initial offering.
>
> (2) An organizational network with the capability to originate loans under competitive conditions and successfully manage them.
>
> (3) Rapid growth potential of portfolio, i.e., a leverage capability.

(4) High indicated return on portfolio, i.e., 10%–12% annual rate for short-term loans; 8½%–10% for permanent mortgages.

(5) Modest premium over book value—thereby allowing the trust to raise additional capital (without diluting book value) and yet not discounting future growth potential. (Not necessary for established trusts).

(6) No trustees affiliated with the parent organization.

(7) Good operating record.

There are other indirect ways to invest in mortgages. One is through the Federal National Mortgage Association ("Fannie Mae") which we met in an earlier chapter. The agency exists to handle mortgages not otherwise insured so as to improve their marketability. There's another arm of the operation called Government National Mortgage Association ("Ginnie Mae" or GNMA). The prospectus explained that FNMA and GNMA "have from time to time entered into agreements to purchase at par or from three to five percentage points below par (depending upon the particular program involved) certain mortgages insured by FHA or guaranteed by VA." These commitments or mortgages are usually assigned or sold to FNMA by GNMA at prevailing market prices.

Investors can buy Fannie Mae common stock and convertible capital debentures for a part of the mortgage action; and Ginnie Mae mortgage-backed securities. They can also buy stocks of mortgage banking companies.

RENTAL REAL ESTATE

"Money from renting a house or apartment? That's for bigger investors than I," one man told me after the subject came up at an investment seminar. I asked how much he had to invest.

"About $2,000," he replied. Our dialog thereafter went something like this:

Q. What is some typical arithmetic?

A. Take a hypothetical case. You have $2,000 to invest. With it, you buy income-producing property costing about $20,000. You give an $18,000 note. Rental income runs about $2,000. This finances notes to the mortgage company and leaves you around

$800 a year for plowback. Assume you escape taxation because the mortgage interest, upkeep costs, etc., are immediately deductible expenses, and with depreciation of the structure on, say, a fifteen-year table (the Treasury might allow this if the building is not new), you have a small net loss which can be used to offset taxes on income from other sources.

You possess the $800 income which accrues after mortgage costs and running expense even though you escape taxation on it. In three years, you have accumulated another $2,400 stake. The depreciation will be used to lessen the taxable cost base of the house and eventually, if you sell it, you will pay capital gains rates on the amount of profit. With $2,400 you go looking for a similar house. Soon, you have two income producers, and shortly you're searching for a third in the form of another income-producing rental house. (Remember that depreciation rules and changing tax laws govern this charge-off situation, and in any given case it's wise to have the advice of a tax professional.)

Q. Suppose I don't have $2,000?

A. The seller might finance part of the cost. Look again at that $20,000 multifamily house. Regular loan sources will provide $18,000. You have only $1,000. ("Here's a sure sale," you may say to the seller, "except for a missing $1,000 to be financed. I'll give you a second mortgage for that amount. You will spread out your receipts from the sale, but nail down the sale itself. A deal?")

Q. Who finances the big part of the package?

A. Regular borrowing sources would be a savings and loan association or a mortgage company. If you want to borrow for a shorter length of time, say five to eight years, a bank might be interested. Sometimes sellers finance the whole package because they can secure interest income larger than they would get from bonds or stocks.

Go back to the $20,000 two-family house. After you have owned it for several years your debt is down from $18,000 to $12,000. Real estate in general has risen in comparison to the shrinking dollar, so that it is now appraised at $25,000. So you have $13,000 "equity" in the building and land. Under most conditions, you could borrow enough to bring the package back to $20,000 and thus have a sizable amount with which to bid for other income-producing real estate on which you expect in a few years to work a similar plowback deal.

Q. How do I find the first house?

A. The same way you'd go house-hunting if you wanted to buy a new home. You can read the want ads and go to look at what is offered. Or you can work through a real estate agent. If you use an agent to buy a house from an owner who isn't already represented by one of these agencies, you're likely to pay more. The agreement always states that the agent's commission is paid by the seller. In practice, the seller has to get more if he sells through a commission agent than if the two of you do business person-to-person.

Q. Would the seller add to the price to pay the agent?

A. Buying real estate isn't like buying a shirt or a suit or a share of stock. It is more like buying a car. People haggle. The asking price is seldom paid in full. Where the seller has to pay agency fees, he has less room to maneuver between what he is asking and the amount he has already decided is rock-bottom.

Q. Cite some rules for success.

A. Success isn't automatic any more than it is in buying stocks or playing hopscotch. You have to have some rules for doing the job. These include:

(1) Go for several units where you can—especially on your second venture. If a single apartment goes tenantless for six months, your rental loss during that time is total. If you own three units and one is vacant, the loss is less.

(2) Don't stint on repair money. A unit that looks good rents quickly—and keeps its tenant.

(3) Go for houses rather than stores. The latter are harder to rent and stay vacant longer when a tenant moves out. The trend to shopping centers hurts chances for renting a single commercial unit.

(4) Don't be a nice-guy landlord. The tenant who misses one payment will have twice as hard a time making two. Relaxed rental payments are a poor way to meet social obligations.

(5) Don't pay more than ten times what you expect to receive each year as rent. In inflationary times, some landlords look for a 12 percent return and seek to buy at eight and one half times annual rent.

Q. How do I find tenants?

A. Mostly by advertising, partly by word-of-mouth spread by satisfied people who rent from you. Where you advertise will depend upon the kind of property and where it is located. Whether the word-of-mouth machine goes into operation will depend upon whether your tenants are part of a closed group (workers at the same plant or office, staff of the same university, etc.) and upon whether they like living in your place.

Take advertising. If you're located where people previously living or working in any area can use your premises, then the newspaper might be your best medium.

If your rental is paid by a plant or school, try media there: bulletin boards, school papers, company or union house organs.

Don't advertise without having someone on hand to show the apartment. An existing tenant might do it for you, with or without a consideration. If he says it is a good place, he'll sound more believable—being presumably, if not always in fact, impartial—than the same spiel from the owner.

People have more time to look on weekends. There will be more competing ads then, but on the old principle that the best place to open a service station is a corner which already has three stations, you'll probably be wise to advertise on the days when the classifieds are crowded with other advertisements.

Most leases run by the month, six months, or year, almost never by the week. The days from the fifteenth to the thirtieth are therefore likely to bring you better results than the first part of a month, when the target is still settled before a color TV in his old place and the moment for paying the rent or moving on seems far off.

Often, but not always, the most expensive advertising medium is the cheapest. Paper A, which charges five times the lineage cost of Paper B, does so, usually, because it can deliver six to ten times the readership.

Q. Can I count on keeping property rented all the time?

A. No—but you can shave the odds against 100 percent rental by taking certain steps, such as:

(1) If you have a large enough rental property, consider a swimming pool. People who live in apartments like to be with other humans. Misanthropes opt for wide-open spaces. If there are enough tenants, cost per rental unit becomes relatively small. "Best $5,000 I ever spent, and only $1,000 of it was in cash; the rest was added to notes," said a 28-year-old landlord who has parlayed a small starting stake into sizable and growing rental

units. "I argued when the architect sketched it in. But no more. We're around 90 percent rented, and competing property with the same features, in a similar neighborhood, runs around 75 percent full."

(2) If property isn't new, then build in charm. Cosmetic repairs such as grillwork, period decor, new bathroom fixtures, and other gimmickry doesn't cost as much as it adds.

(3) Take cognizance of the view. If your structure is sited among handsome surroundings, play it up. If it looks over brick kilns or semi-slums and the city dump is a visible half-mile away, use shrubbery to hide the nearby nuisances and windowless walls to avoid seeing those far off.

(4) Conveniences such as coin-op washers and driers, vending machines, etc., add to the usefulness of the building and to the net profit as well. To avoid cheapening the place, put them in a basement or detached outbuilding.

Q. What sort of neighborhood is best?

A. One preferably on the way up, certainly not one degenerating down to semicommercial or rooming houses. Look for an area with a preponderance of younger families. You'll stay more easily rented that way than in an area where the tenants are only occupying space before getting ready to move into a retirement village.

Examine some of the surrounding structures. Are they well maintained? Lawns mowed? Trash picked up? Are the buildings freshly painted? When there are one or two rundown places, the rot soon spreads to other houses; good tenants move away on expiration of their leases and landlords, to stay rented, move down the dollar scale.

Seek an area around public facilities, close to churches and schools, near public transportation. Transportation may not be found in a suburb except in the form of freeways, but if you have other features, you can let that go, since people who like the suburbs also like to go by gasoline.

Last, check zoning board and city planning commission rules. If your plan is to convert an old single into four apartments, make sure you can do it legally before inking your name onto an act of sale that makes you the owner of a house you can live in but can't rent out.

Chapter 14

THE LEAKY TAX SHELTER

The scheme for getting rich that contributed more to investor poverty than any other during the hectic last part of the decade of the sixties was the limited partnership. Some operated in oil drilling, others were set up to raise cattle and horses. Some tree farmed. Some planted and hoped to harvest citrus and other fruits. All had a common setup and three common aims: (1) to shelter some of the investor's income from the sight and grab of the income tax collector; (2) hopefully to make some capital gains for him; and (3) to make money for the promoter.

In some instances, the limited tax shelter partnerships failed in all three aims. Many failed in the first two. Most were successful in the third.

WHAT TAX SHELTERS ARE

A common denominator of tax shelters is organization. The investor purchases "units," "participations," or "partnerships" in multiples of set units. A typical shelter would be an organization with units coming at $2,500, $5,000, $7,500, $10,000, and so on.

The tax shelter usually aims to produce some sizable paper losses at first, which furnish an investor with red-ink entries to reduce the tax he pays on other income or to render tax-free some of the income from the shelter itself. For that reason, the appeal of tax shelters is strongest to investors in the higher tax brackets to whom this kind of saving can be both real and sizable. How it works was explained in the brochure of a cattle partnership promotion:

> A limited partnership is a hybrid form of business organization which combines some of the characteristics of a corporation, but predominately resembles a general partnership. The principal characteristics which liken a limited partnership to a corporation are the centralization of management in the general partner and the participation of the limited partners as passive investors, like shareholders, who risk only their investments. The characteristics of a limited partnership which generally result in its treatment as a partnership for tax purposes are the personal liability of the general partner for the debts of the partnership, the lack of free transferability of partnership interests, and the limited duration of the life of the partnership.

> . . . In general, in the cattle feeding phase of the cattle business, feed costs and other expenses will be allowed as ordinary deductions during the year in which payment is made, and profits from the sale of feeder cattle will be treated as ordinary income in the year in which payment is received. Advance purchases of feed, in reasonable amounts, may be deducted for income tax purposes in the accounting period during which payment is made, but advance payments for services to be rendered in later accounting periods are not deductible until the services are performed.

> Gains or losses from the sale of cattle which are held for breeding purposes, if held for more than 24 months, will be treated as long-term capital gains or losses. However, sales of calves from a breeding herd generally produce ordinary income.

In this instance, the partnership is expected to generate both ordinary income and eventual capital gains. Most participation deals look for this. Some put varying emphasis on production of ordinary income which it is hoped to make nontaxable to some extent, and on capital gains, taxed at rates lower than ordinary income. In many the start-up and other costs are immediately deductible. To the investor in a lofty tax bracket, this becomes important; he is able sometimes to recoup his entire investment quickly out of saved income tax, the participation remaining afterward as gravy. Said one former Securities and Exchange Commission staff member who moved into the lucrative field of tax shelter promotion: "Because of . . . lack of liquidity, the object of oil investment should be to reduce your investment to zero as fast as possible. Once you've got your money back, you can start worrying about making a profit."

The high-bracket investor obviously gets his money back faster than the investor in lower brackets. To the latter, the appeal of limited partnership participations is less inviting. The arithmetic was explained in an article entitled "Should You Invest in an Oil Drilling Program?" which appeared in the June 22, 1970, issue of *Medical Economics*:

> Let's say, for example, that you're in the 50 per cent bracket and you invest $10,000 in an oil drilling fund. Generally, about two-thirds of the amount an oil program spends to put down each well is intangible drilling expense. This means that $6,700 or so of your $10,000 investment can be deducted from your income. Since you're in the 50 per cent bracket, you'll save $3,350 in taxes, so the cost of your $10,000 investment will, in effect, be cut rapidly to $6,650. Through depreciation of capital equipment and write-off of proven acreage, the remaining one-third of your investment will eventually be deductible from your income, saving you an additional $1,650 in taxes.
>
> The higher your tax bracket, clearly, the less your investment actually costs you and the more your risk is reduced.

Minerals programs differ from oil-drilling operations in that they search for and expect to sell ores at a profit, rather than petroleum. Their tax advantages are minimally different in some cases because of changed depletion allowances.

LEVERAGE

Leverage is inherent in all types of tax shelter partnerships. Leverage, discussed in regard to orthodox investing in an earlier chapter, allows moderate money to swing investments of larger-than-moderate size. Leverage is great when it works; if all goes well, the investor of small financial stature is quickly able to build himself into a big-time operator. When all does not happen as the original game plan said it should, then the leverage produces losses.

In a few cases, an investor can purchase participations valued at thousands of dollars with no cash outlay at all. The president of a citrus investment company wrote to me that "Initial cash requirements may be borrowed, using our banking connections, with repayment predicated on the tax refund due you as a result of having made a citrus investment this year."

For this kind of leverage, an investor might pay heavily, but if the investment seems sound, the heavy cost might be worth acceptance.

THE DRAWBACKS

Because tax shelters have been widely promoted, little understood, and frequently a source of short-term losses to disappointed investors who, if they had understood their commitments and hung on sufficiently long, would have fared well in the end, it is necessary to understand the unfavorable side of the shelter medium.

Contract Favoring Promoter The first drawback is a contract which almost guarantees promoters' profit, often at the expense of the shelter seeker. A prospectus for Apache Land Grove Program 1970 listed the kinds, ways, and manners in which the seller of partnerships expected to gain:

As general partner, Apache is entitled to three kinds of compensation.

The first is a *one-third share* of the annual net operating cash income from each parcel of land after the participants in the Program have earned a 12% return that year on their undepreciated capital investment in the parcel.

"Net operating cash income" is defined in the articles to mean cash income minus operating expenses, *exclusive of debt service and depreciation.* "Capital investment" is defined to mean the cumulative capital outlay on any parcel, *exclusive of interest paid,* before the first year in which the parcel produces net operating cash income. Once a parcel is generating net operating cash income the capital investment changes only if capital additions to or subtractions from the parcel are made.

. . . The second form of compensation to the general partner is a one-fourth share in the proceeds from the sale or exchange of any parcel at a gain over the Program's capital investment in the parcel, before the deduction of any depreciation.

The third is a management fee of 3% of the proceeds of this or any subsequent offering of Program units. This is to compensate the general partner for supervising the investment of the offering proceeds to achieve the objectives of the Program.

In addition to these, profit may be earned by Apache as manager of the ranch, rather than as general partner, under the care and management contract. (Italics supplied.)

Inept Management Although many managements (Apache, for example, up to the time of this writing) provided for their fees capable, professional management, others proved inept and for high fees investors bought only poor performance. Examples were King Resources in the petroleum field and Black Watch Farms in the cattle area.

In each of these, existing management had spent heavily on entertaining prospective investors, with more effort put into selling its capabilities than in exercise of those capabilities for the limited partners' benefit. Later, managements were forced out but that did not save investors from heavy losses.

In the 1970 annual report of King Resources, parent and partner of King operating partnerships, the new Chief Operating Officer who replaced earlier management was frank in his explanation of what had happened:

> Many of you have asked what has happened. It is impossible to give a simple answer to a very complex set of circumstances. However, in essence, in May of 1970 the Company became involved in an unsuccessful attempt to take over control of I.O.S. Ltd. Approximately $16,000,-000 of Company funds were utilized in connection with the takeover attempt. As a consequence, severe liquidity problems developed. Coincident with this action, entities managed by I.O.S. Ltd., which previously were major customers of the Company, ceased investing in new exploration programs with the Company. At approximately the same time, subsidiaries of The Colorado Corporation, which had also been major customers, ceased doing business with the Company. A summary of the I.O.S. Ltd. takeover attempt will be included in the Company's proxy statement which should be forwarded to you in the very near future.
>
> In addition, the Company has become involved in a substantial amount of litigation, including two actions by the Securities and Exchange Commission against the Company alleging, among other things, violations of Federal securities laws in connection with the I.O.S. Ltd. takeover attempt and in connection with borrowings made by the Company from the State of Ohio.

This statement was sent to stockholders of the parent firm who watched their publicly-traded stock plummet. They were luckier than participants in King drilling programs. The stockholders were able to sell, even at losses, and so recoup part of their original capital. Limited partners frequently could not realize the remaining value at all.

Like King, Black Watch, in its days of high riding, was the leading outfit in its corral. At the peak, Black Watch managed 30,000 head of investors' cattle in more than three-score spreads over twenty states. Leading figures from advertising, show biz, the professions, and the ranks of industrial leadership "owned" these cattle and later watched them rustled away. The company became involved with legal difficulties, some brought on by New York State's attorney general, and at this writing is insolvent.

Uninformed Investors Investors absorbed sizable losses in drilling, cattle-feeding, and citrus-growing partnerships partly because they did not understand the dangers and the fact that, like stock or real estate investments, these can go down as well as up—with their losses compounded by nonliquidity.

Most partnership prospectuses warn frankly of this. Eager seekers of tax shelter could be saved later disappointment and loss if they read paragraphs such as the following from the offering literature of Apache Land Grove Program 1970:

> There will be no public market for Program units. A limited number are being offered and the transferability of units is limited. The Program or Apache Corporation may purchase units from investors who wish to sell but cannot find a buyer. *However, neither the Program nor Apache has any obligation to buy any units, and even if they do the price is 75% of the unit's appraised value.* No assurance is made that investors will be able to sell their units to third parties or to the Program or Apache.
>
> An investor who subscribes for a full Program unit commits himself to pay $20,000 over a term ending in 1974. If he subscribes for a half unit, he agrees to pay $10,000 by that time. These are the amounts put at risk when an investor agrees to participate in this Program, unless the general partner elects to permit him to remain in the Program with an interest limited to the amount actually paid on the purchase price. This procedure is optional with the general partner and is subject to limitations. . . . *An investor who fails to pay the full subscription price of the unit purchased may be subject to legal proceedings to enforce that obligation.* (Italics supplied.)

Additional Assessments A partner in a tax shelter program can frequently be assessed additional amounts on top of the sums he thought were maximum input. From the prospectus of White Shield Oil and Gas Exploratory Fund Series A:

> Following expenditure of the Participant's subscription increments paid over to a Drilling Partnership, further

expenditures may prove necessary to further develop Drilling Blocks acquired during the Drilling Partnership's period of Primary Operations. Such further development will be financed to the maximum extent possible by the use of Drilling Partnership revenues, or the sale or pledge as collateral against loans, of its assets. To the extent further moneys are required, such development costs will be borne by those "Affected Participants" electing to participate in such operations. Affected Participants electing not to participate will receive an overriding revenue interest equal to their proportionate part of 6¼% of Drilling Partnership revenues attributable to the operation, free and clear of all costs and expenses other than taxes. The remaining revenues will be credited to Participants participating in the cost of the operation in the ratio in which such costs were shared by them.

Election by a Participant not to participate in such a "Further Operation" will increase both the percentage of the costs and the percentage of the revenues to be borne and received by those Participants who do participate in the operation. The non-consenting Participants will receive their overriding revenue interest on the revenues from this operation; however, this interest will be substantially less than the share of the revenues they would have received from such operation if they had participated therein.

THE ADVANTAGES

The advantages of tax shelters are solid and sound. The partnerships' greatest applicability is to investors who find that their other incomes place them in high tax brackets and who are thus able to write off substantial investing costs out of tax savings. They have attraction—less, but real—to investors in lower brackets who are fascinated with owning a piece of a well or a share of a prize bull, or who like the idea of drawing wealth from the land and enjoying a tax write-off of some of the income.

Not all partnership managers have proved inept as were those who ran Black Watch and King Resources. Not all partnerships have provision for further assessment of participants and, where these exist, they are not always disadvantageous to the investor (provided he has the necessary money to put up and wishes to do so). Not all management fees are set up to benefit the general partners more than the limited partners, although in this area it is much more the rule than the exception that general partners benefit whether things go well or badly, whereas they have to go well for the limited partners to come out ahead. A few partnerships make genuine efforts to find markets for the participation units of investors who want out or who require the funds; none, however, guarantee to do so.

On the plus side is the expertise of management which is as necessary to farming as the earth itself, and as vital in drilling as the existence of oil on land being explored. Not all managements possess ability of a high grade. But neither do the managements of corporations whose stock an investor might buy or mutual funds in whose shares he might invest.

When things work out as planned, a participation should liquidate its cost and still leave the investor an operating entity. That is the biggest advantage of all.

Chapter 15

POINTS TO REMEMBER

$\left(\mathbf{1}\right)$ In the 1969–1970 decline, growth stocks dropped twice—often four and five times—as far and as fast as did the general stock market. By 1971, average stock prices had recovered close to their earlier high levels. Not so the growth stocks. Many of these showed only minimal recovery. The same was true of mutual funds devoted to wild in-out speculation in these stocks.

(2) Many of the values on which highly-touted growth was based turned out to be questionable and at least some of the "earnings" and other figures shown by growth corporations were based upon outright juggling. Investors learned that books can be made—at least for a time—to say whatever the bookkeepers want them to indicate.

(3) Inflation had proved a factor in the growth and later in the death of the growth concept. Investors should not again be deluded into a belief that inflation can bring about good effects on stocks or the corporate profits and assets behind stock prices.

(4) Investors were not the only victims of the growth mania. Wall Street itself suffered. Many of its prestigious old brokerage names vanished into bankruptcy or continued to appear in com-

pany names only as part of the titles of sounder firms with which they had merged. Francis I. duPont and Co. and Glore Forgan became one, Goodbody and Company vanished into the firm of Merrill Lynch, Pierce, Fenner and Smith without survival of as much as a part of its name. Out of this string of bankruptcies and failures, investors learned that their funds were better kept in insured bank accounts than with their brokers, and that the best way to keep securities was to hold them in safe deposit boxes.

(5) Some mutual funds proved no safer from manipulation of the figures than some corporations. By means of "letter stocks," some growth-oriented mutual funds managed to make their net-asset values per share seem to appreciate sharply when in reality they were not doing so or were even dropping in value. From this, investors should learn, even though the letter-stock gambit has been severely circumscribed by new SEC rules, to examine all components of a fund's portfolio.

(6) The emphasis on constant growth of stocks will be replaced with emphasis on how well a corporation fulfills social needs. Today, the social emphasis is on better living in our cities and better ecological practices outside them. Tomorrow, the emphasis may shift as problems are solved or new ones arise. The important thing is to know what the problems are and to identify the companies engaged in solving them.

(7) Yet, reliance must be placed on corporation books, too: Study the balance sheet. A company having a higher book value than price is said to be worth more dead than alive. Such a situation often attracts conglomerates or others who feel they can put poorly used assets to efficient employment. Investors can gain when their buying brings up the price of such a stock. A firm with quick assets—cash, immediate receivables, and things such as government bonds which are equivalent to cash—greater than the price of the stock becomes a particularly attractive target and hence often a particularly profitable investment.

(8) Instead of aiming at forever growth as investors did in the sixties, investors of the seventies can profitably use parlaying and plowback. Parlaying comes about when the profits from one investment are reinvested in toto in the next. Plowback calls for reinvesting all dividends, interest, and so forth from an investment so that these are added to capital and begin to generate

new dividends or interest on their own, which can then be added to capital and the process endlessly repeated.

(9) "Insiders" are those possessed of knowledge not known yet by the public. They include officers and directors of a company and those who beneficially own more than 10 percent of its stock. Following what they do furnishes investors of the seventies a way to act with the insiders even though unaware of the exact facts which led the insiders in question to buy or sell the stock. The transactions of insiders are, by law, reported to the Securities and Exchange Commission which then publishes them in a monthly report available to the public.

(10) An old analytical technique which is coming back and which will be usful to investors in the decade ahead is the assets-in-the-ground approach. It calls for study of reserve assets such as oil and iron ore, still in the ground. Study of the stocks comprising the Dow Jones Industrial Average showed that investment in the ones which owned assets in the ground turned out to be more profitable than investment in the general group comprising the Average itself.

(11) A ploy which always works, but is difficult to apply, is investment in sound, brainy managements which will make a company succeed over competitors whose guiding group is less aggressive or less wise.

(12) Trends in stock favor or in economic needs often go on for lengthy periods. An example was the rise in steel capacity and use and in the prices of steel stocks during the fifties. Another was the rise of leisure-oriented stocks in the sixties. Correctly analyzing trends and investing in accordance with them will be a way to make profitable investments in the seventies as well.

(13) Everybody seeks popularity, not least corporate officers who want their stocks to bask in the sunshine of investor favor in order to facilitate financing as well as to lift the values of their personal holdings of their companies' stocks. But unpopularity can pay off. Studies have shown that buying stocks after actions which induce unpopularity (running a deficit instead of a profit, reducing or dropping a dividend) often lead to long-term investment profits. Stocks bought at such a time are at their cheapest, and any improvement can lift their prices spectacularly. This will not cease to be so in the seventies.

(14) Blue-chip stocks have the ability to survive storms which would wreck—and in 1969–1970 did wreck—many "blue-sky" companies. Investment in the blue chips is likely to be profitable in the decade ahead, since vulnerability of fragile, poorly-based stocks was revealed clearly after the death of the growthomania.

(15) The interest of investors and the tides of business success rotate among blue chips and mutual funds. The stock or fund which leads the pack one year may trail it the next. Such investments should be reevaluated regularly.

(16) Bonds and other kinds of income-producing investments will give greater opportunity than heretofore as their solid merits emerge. Income investment media include preferred stocks, some mutual funds devoted to production of income for their shareowners, high-yield common stocks, and—under some circumstances discussed earlier—banks' Certificates of Deposit. Prices of income investments can fluctuate, too, and a knowledge based on observation of money-market conditions helps to determine the best times to buy and the times of easy money and high bond prices when these investments can be wisely sold. There are bonds whose incomes are exempt from Federal taxes and, in some cases, from taxation in the state where they were issued as well. These are particularly useful to investors in higher income brackets where the tax savings become substantial. Some bonds and preferred stocks afford a way to play both ends of the market. They are convertible at holders' option into common stock so that the income from them can be enjoyed; if the company prospers and the common stock rises in price, the option to convert can then be exercised.

(17) In the seventies inflation won't stop, although it may abate from time to time as governmental efforts made to contain it sometimes partially succeed. Wage and price controls won't go entirely off in the foreseeable future, although they may considerably diminish. The U.S. dollar will stay in trouble, with additional devaluations of the dollar and more realignments vis-à-vis foreign currencies probably coming. The influence of the monetary school of economists will probably diminish. A depression could hit America and the rest of the world. But from this sea of troubles and worries will arise a new prosperity, hopefully

free of some of the excesses of the sixties. *This new prosperity will present investors with opportunity to grow very rich.*

(18) North Americans tend to think of investing opportunity as being concentrated in the United States and Canada. This is not so; some other nations' economies are prospering at a better rate than here, and the ways of investing in them are as easy as investing in a stateside or Canadian stock. An investor can also participate in foreign opportunity by investment in foreign currencies and certain "multinational" United States stocks.

(19) There are times when short-term investing is needful, as an investor waits out turn of adverse trends or when he employs funds which will be available on only a temporary basis. Good temporary investment vehicles include Treasury Bills, semi-government corporations' paper, Certificates of Deposit, commercial paper, and even, for the wealthy, tax-exempt short-term notes, sometimes through Eurodollars.

(20) To all of us, the day comes when we leave work and head, hopefully, toward a pleasant retirement. Developments among private pension funds threaten this outlook. Social Security alone won't provide enough. The investor himself has to do something. He should, if self-employed, look into the advantages of a Keogh plan. During pre-retirement years he can accumulate capital through investments and, if the income such capital generates is not sufficient, he can make partial withdrawals from the capital periodically after retirement. With a self-investment plan or by means of a pension plus Social Security plus insurance, an overall long-range plan is needed which will take cognizance of adverse possibilities in addition to the profit angles.

(21) The seventies will not be free of bear markets. These seem to come at shorter intervals than they did under our fathers' investing conditions, and they last shorter periods of time after they do come. A reason may be the increase in big institutional investors such as mutual funds, banks, insurance companies, and pension funds, and the degree to which their activities now dominate the investing scene. With the bear markets coming around faster, it is important to recognize the advent of one, if possible before it hits and at any event not too long after the peak of the old bull market. The re-study methods that experts

have worked out are in many ways better than the old methods of studying bull-bear trends, since, being new, they are not yet widely followed. A market testing tool which is followed by a great number of investors tends to become self-defeating, as all act together on the signals. During bear trends, either sell short (if you wish to participate actively with the down trends as well as within the up trends), or hold money off the market by investing in short-term paper. *In either case, the course of wisdom, once an investor becomes convinced that a new bear market has arrived, is to sell out all stocks while waiting for a more propitious time to reinvest.*

(22) Investors will find new ways during the seventies to put capital into the oldest investment medium—real estate. The opportunities will be great, as an expected new wave of family formations and of births creates need for land use. Among ways available is the Real Estate Investment Trust which, like the stock mutual fund, gives an investor diversification along with professional management of his property portfolio. Once denied access to the rich-yield mortgage market, ordinary investors can now participate through some of these REIT's which specialize in mortgages, through stock in the Federal National Mortgage Association ("Fannie Mae") and paper of the Government National Mortgage Association ("Ginnie Mae"). Rental real estate is within the means of many and can bring rich returns.

(23) But one medium, popular in the late part of the sixties, entails danger. This is the "tax shelter." The group comprises petroleum limited partnerships, and other limited partnerships in citrus growing, cattle growing, and almond groves. Tax shelters offer diversification plus professional management and aim at generating tax *losses* in initial years. A corollary of this is that the appeal should only be to investors in higher tax brackets to whom such a loss is a meaningful amount and not a mere small book-keeping entry.

INDEX